THE PERIODIC TABLE

★ ★ ★ ★ ★ OF ★ ★ ★ ★ ★

MILITARY TRANSITION

The Elements of Success

THE TRANSITIONING MILITARY SERIES

THE PERIODIC TABLE

★ ★ ★ ★ ★ OF ★ ★ ★ ★ ★

MILITARY TRANSITION

The Elements of Success

Jay Hicks, PMP
Lieutenant Colonel, United States Army, Retired

THE TRANSITIONING MILITARY SERIES

Published by

GR8TRANSITIONS4U

GR8TRANSITIONS4U (USA) Inc.

Palmetto, Florida 34221

USA

Copyright © 2022, Jay Hicks

Hicks, Jay

THE PERIODIC TABLE OF MILITARY TRANSITION

ISBN 978-1-7343933-4-7

Printed in the United States of America

Book design by Tamara Parsons

GR8Transitions4U.com

Endorsements

A MUST read BEFORE you even think about transitioning from the military to the civilian workforce; then keep for the resources! Clear and concisely written, filled with real-world examples from the Veterans who began FEDEX and the Black Rifle Coffee Company along with a plethora of resources to dig deeper as you begin the high adventure of military TRANSITION. Only wished it had been around during my transition; it would've saved me years in discovery learning! About time, Jay.

Cindy Gaddis, PMP
SVP, Business Development

Over the past few years, I have worked with LTC (R) Jay Hicks on various projects while a member of the Project Management Institute (PMI) the premier professional organization for Project Management profession. The culmination of Jay's efforts over the past decade and his Transitioning Military Book series assisting active duty, veterans, contractors, and civilian personnel has resulted in his latest brilliant creation of the Periodic Table of Military Transition (PTMT). Just as the Periodic Table of Elements is a system of arranging chemical elements that make up the basic substances of all matter, Jay has developed a system of basic elements in his Periodic Table of Military Transition for a successful transition from the military to a satisfying civilian career. As a fellow veteran who has gone through the difficult transition from a 30-year military & engineering profession to a successful Project Management civilian career, I wish I had available an effective and concise tool such as the PTMT. The PTMT would have made my transition from active duty to a project management career less stressful, much easier, and more effective. Thank you to Jay and his group for putting such a useful, professional, and essential tool such as the PTMT!

COL (R) Aldo (Al) R. Calvi PMP, PE
Past PMI Region 14 Mentor

Dedicated to the
Soldiers, Marines, Sailors, and Airmen
of the United States Military.

Table of Contents

Pre-Transition Factors

1.0 - Market:

2.0 - Environment:

3.0 - Personal Trait Awareness:

4.0 - Transferable Skills:

5.0 - Tools:

6.0 - Civilian Integration:

Post-Transition Factors

7.0 - Professional Development:

Foreword

You have made the decision to get out of the military. Now you need to develop your transition plan from the military and figure out how to combine your years of military experience, Service, and training to help you enter the next phase of your life. Jay's book is based on his experiences of going from a soldier to a civilian and is providing you with the *Periodic Table of Military Transition* to help you in this process. The Periodic Table navigates you from your military life enabling a smooth transition into the civilian world. Jay provides you the ingredients to become an alchemist, mixing the basic elements of your current experience together to make the compounds that optimize your movement from being a service member to a civilian.

In the 36 years I have known Jay, he has always helped others. From our time together as young Lieutenants, I could see his passion for helping. During our first tour together at Fort Leonard Wood, Missouri, Jay made it a point to be there for the soldiers, helping them learn their new individual skills. In later years when assigned to Germany, Fort Hood, Texas and then Central Command (CENTCOM) Headquarters in Tampa, Jay remained concerned with helping soldiers to take care of themselves and their families.

This book, like Jay's other books in *The Transitioning Military Series*, are designed to help soldiers transition their military skills into civilian specialties, along with providing insight into becoming certified Program Management

Professionals (PMP). Your military skills are very similar, and some are the same as those used by PMP's. These other publications help you see how valuable your military skills are outside of the military.

We are both logistics soldiers whose profession was to take care of others we supported, and Jay has taken this a step further by carrying on his support of services members as they transition into the civilian world. As a retired Army Colonel, I wish there had been a book like this to help guide me through the transitioning process. I commend Jay for having the foresight to want to help those service members who came after us, and not make the same mistakes we made in our transitions. Because of Jay's concern for our service members, I recommend all his books to all those I meet so they can transition from the military and apply their experiences to the skills used in the civilian world.

The Periodic Table of Military Transition is a great book designed to remove the intimidation associated with taking the big transition step away from the military and into the civilian workforce. Jay's book should be provided to all service members who go through the Transition Assistance Program, as it would make the entire process even easier. A must read for all enlisted and officers who are transitioning.

Thanks Jay!

COL F. Keith Jones, USA, Ret, PMP
President at SAWTST, LLC

About the Book

Great Job! If you are looking at this book, you are probably in the throes of military transition. This book provides a springboard for your preparation. In *The Periodic Table of Military Transition*, you will find the essential elements for your successful military transition. These elements were derived over time with your success in mind. My desire is to provide you with great information for your transition, as your need for quality insight and information is crucial during this period in your life.

With your success in mind, *The Periodic Table of Military Transition* enables learning by providing essential information through an easily digestible format. Within this book, you will find a collection of topics organized as elements in a periodic table. Each element is carefully selected and derived through experiences and interaction with transitioning military personnel.

The elements are arranged in seven distinct columns or element groups. The first four element groups assist in personal awareness, as you must know about yourself and your preparedness to begin the transition. The next two groups are about the development of essential tools and networks. A final column on post-transition factors is provided for follow on workplace development.

After many years of combined service on active duty, as defense contractor, and military transition specialist, my experiences provide a significant understanding of the challenges associated with military transition. I enjoy speaking and assisting military personnel in transition just like you, receiving significant satisfaction helping veterans and military personnel with their personal journeys. I continue to produce a tremendous amount of written material about the topic and I urge you to follow me on social media.

If you find this book helpful during your successful transition, please let me know and give this book to others so that they might use it. This mission is truly about helping others make the transition and avoiding many of the common transitional pitfalls.

Thank you for your service. Now it is time for your speedy and successful transition.

Jay Hicks

THE PERIODIC TABLE
of
MILITARY TRANSITION

Introduction

You are not alone! As you begin your journey, know that millions of service members have already transitioned successfully. In fact, 18 million or about 7% of the population has served in the military. Historically, nearly 100 million men and women have made the same successful journey you are about to make.

This introduction will require some introspection. Simple questions are asked, and you need to review and think through the answers. This will pay dividends as you progress through *The Periodic Table of Military Transition.*

The 5Ws

Your military transition starts with the "5Ws." You know how to analyze the 5Ws from your military experience. Now it is time to consider the "5Ws" with regard to your personal transitional journey.

Why?

Have you thought about "Why" are you leaving the service? Are you getting out just because your contract is finished? For various reasons, many service members have decided they must get out, seldom thinking about "Why." Without this exercise, you could exert tremendous effort, for little Return on Investment (ROI). Think about: Why do I believe that I am heading towards a better career? What do I really want to do on the outside? Do I believe my current benefits and military career are not as good as my potential future career? Asking yourself these questions and thinking about the answers may help you assess your current and future situation more clearly.

What is the What?

Have you thought about the "What" your new career after the military will be? You need to know the "What" before your transition date. Do you have the Knowledge, Skills and Abilities (KSAs) to perform the "What"? Do you need to go back to school? Have you begun to develop a brand? Can you use the "What" you already know and re-engineer yourself? If you have not decided on the "What," consider reading *The Transitioning Combat Arms Professional*, written for all military personnel.

Who? *You've* Got to Do It!

The "Who" is You! If you are coming up short on skills, training or education; you will have to do what it takes to become a competitive new you. Do you need certifications? Classes? Licenses? Maybe you just need to gain an understanding of project management, SAP®, video editing, Microsoft Office, or SolarWinds® products. There is a wealth of information available on-line for skills training, enabled through video and white papers. If you must go deep, there has never been a better time. Today, there have never been more methods and offerings so many offerings by numerous organizations trying to assist veterans. Further, the G.I Bill is better and easier to use than ever before in the history of the program.

Where?

There are lots of considerations beyond physical or geographic locations. Rather than just going back to your home of record, elements such as finance, taxes, commute, and family must be considered in post military location decision making. We will dig into these later. Just understand you need to do some serious thinking about "Where" you will move to.

How? (Not a W....)

When you know "What" you are going to do, then you are ready for the "How."

The "How" requires such activities as developing a personal brand, enhancing your network, selecting experienced mentors early, and studying transition materials; all of which are discussed later.

Also, the "How" requires a plan or a personal strategic roadmap. Write your goals and objectives down on paper. Break the objectives down further into tasks. Refer to these often and make sure you stay on track. The "How" success rate climbs, if you can have an accountability partner, which could be a mentor, a spouse, or anyone that will challenge you to stay on track. For more information, check out Gr8Transitions4U.com Knowledge Center for a copy of the Personal Strategic Roadmap.

Ready, Set, Go! (The When)

"When" you have a brand and web presence and "When" your advocates know what you are doing and "When" you are networked, you are ready to begin your job search.

First, is your Social Media working for or against you? Are you portraying the new you? Or are you portraying the "military you"? Does your resume reflect your professional social media account? Your brand recognition is based on what you are good at and what you desire to do.

Second, make sure your advocates work for you. They want to help. Do these wonderful people know "What" your plans and desires are? Think about "How" they can help and make sure they understand their special role.

You owe it to yourself to find professionals that can help you. Make new contacts. Join professional organizations, volunteer, and seek a mentor. People can be very generous if you have the right approach and they feel that they can help you. Ask for advice and thank them. By staying in touch with them, you will enable new lifelong friendships with professionals in the field you desire to transition. Remember that a job search can be a full-time job in itself. Have a battle rhythm or regular schedule for your job search.

Change or Transition?

The difference between change and transition is subtle, but important. Change is something that happens to you, even if you don't like it. Transition, on the other hand, is internal. It is what happens in your mind as you go through change. Change can happen very quickly, while transition usually occurs more slowly.

Our lives are full of change, and your military transition will prove to be one of your greatest challenges and achievements. How will you handle this change? Are you going to be frustrated or will you be tossed about like a boat in a storm?

> *"It isn't the changes that do you in; it's the transitions."*
>
> ~ WILLIAM BRIDGES

Your attitude can lead to resistance and opposition during the transition, after the change. To transition successfully you must embrace your personal change and mentally take charge of your transition. Use your knowledge and experience to embrace your personal and professional change.

In today's challenging work environment, you must be flexible, able to embrace change and continually transition to remain viable. The good news is your military experience has instilled the ability to adapt to ever changing environments. This flexibility will serve you well as you respond to change. As you depart the Service, remember to embrace the associated changes, but remain focused on your transition.

Companies are seeking qualified candidates with your abilities. If you have met your personal military objectives and are ready to transition to the rapidly changing commercial work environment, this is all good news for you.

A Couple of Words on Intimidation

Some may feel intimidated by the upcoming transition. A friend once told me that diametrically opposed behaviors can impede those desiring careers or professions in fields such as music, art, sports, etc. I believe this applies to military service members and their transition.

Some military personnel already know what they are going to do professionally after the military. However, many service members have not given transition much thought. Lacking a destination can be very intimidating.

For some, this intimidation is based on fear of the unknown. These reservations are often due to a lack of transitional knowledge; including selection of a commercial career field, putting together resumes, cover letters, professional branding and/or surviving the interview.

When a lack of information or understanding is blocking the path, creativity can be inhibited. Service members can become fixated on the "next steps" and fail to look at the big picture. The transition may become intimidating and procrastination may set in. Waiting has proven to be dangerous and often creates undesirable results.

What if you are in a similar situation? You have made a great choice picking up this book as working through *The Periodic Table of Military Transition* will provide confidence for your journey. Just like your physical training, start a personal self-awareness and education program. Read transitional books on various career fields of interest, such as Information Technology (IT), project management, and logistics. Gr8Transitions4U has a variety of topical transition books. You may not select any of these fields, but studying various occupations enhances your aspirations.

If you are significantly intimidated and have no idea what career field to pursue, try reading books like Dick Bolles' *What Color is Your Parachute?* or *The Transitioning Combat Arms Professional*. Both books provide practical information for job hunters and career changers; with *The Transitioning Combat Arms Professional* being tailored specifically for military service members, regardless of your branch of Service.

Once you have begun self-education, seek out professionals in the commercial career field you are leaning toward. How? Join a professional networking group such as PMI®, Toastmasters®, Rotary, Optimists or Business Networking International (BNI). Here you will find civilians that will be interested in helping you make your transition. You might even find a mentor.

These first few initial steps will assist in reducing your intimidation and optimistically enable your creativity while simultaneously motivating your transitional journey.

About the Periodic Table of Military Transition

The Periodic Table of Military Transition (Appendix A) provides a method for your successful transition, borrowing the familiar periodic structure used in chemistry and physics. Each block in the table represents an element of transition. Each element has a background chapter providing key information on that focus area.

Many of the elements are under your control during and after your transition from the military. Elements not under your control are risk areas. These elements must be analyzed and reviewed periodically, with work arounds established.

Element Periods

Within *The Periodic Table of Military Transition*, each element belongs to one of three periods. The periods are color-coded BLUE, GREEN and RED. The first period grouping is made up of pre-transition factors and is color coded BLUE. The elements should be personally analyzed and processed prior to your transition.

The second period group represents post-transition factors and are color coded in GREEN. Once you have transitioned, these professional development elements should continually be worked and improved.

Elements in RED represent personal transitional study that you have not yet completed. These shortcomings are potential caution areas and need your attention prior to transition.

Element Groups

Each element is also arranged into columns or groupings. Elements from the same column group of the periodic table have similar characteristics. There are a total of seven column groups: Marketing, Environment, Personal Traits,

Transferable Skills, Tools, Civilian Network, and Development. The first six groups are those things that should be accomplished prior to your transition. The last column group of elements will assist your professional development after career transition.

Naming Convention

Each element is noted by two letters; the first letter represents the element group and the second represents the topic of the element. You will find the element name listed in the Table of Contents and on the Table in Appendix A.

Numeric System

The numeric system associated with the elements displays a small number in the top right-hand corner of each element. As you read and analyze each element's chapter, consider your situation, and make personal change as necessary. Track of your development through scoring yourself against each element, focusing on the areas you find most challenging. As you progress, calculate, and keep track of your total score. When you achieve a score of 90 or above you are probably ready to begin your transitional journey. Use the elements from this table as a guide for your transitional preparation progress.

If you have found this book after your transition has begun, you will still find the information and introspective questions valuable during your transition. However, the post-transition factors will provide meaningful assistance for you, throughout your career

As with the Periodic Table of the Elements used for chemistry and physics, *The Periodic Table of Military Transition* will continue to evolve as trends in the job market and changes to the military departure process occur.

The Periodic Table

PRE-TRANSITION FACTOR AWARENESS

MARKET

Ma   Analysis

Mp   Personal Desires

Mc   Companies Selection

Xm   Job Market Understanding

ENVIRONMENT

Et   Timing

Ef   Family

Eb   Benefits/Financial

El   Location

Xe   No Personal Analysis

PERSONAL TRAITS

Pl   Leader

Pv   Vocation

Pw   Work-Life Balance

Pd   Discipline Competition

Pc   Competition Unawarness

Xp   Lack of Awarness

TRANSFERABLE SKILLS

Sc   Certification

Se   Education

Sx   Experience

Xs   Unrealized Skills

The **Periodic Table of Military Transition** provides a method for your successful transition. **BLUE** elements should be analyzed and worked during your transition. Those elements in **GREEN** enable your successes after transition. Elements in **RED** represent shortcomings needing correction.

PRE **TRANSITION**

MARKET	ENVIRONMENTAL	PERSONAL TRAITS
Ma +5	Et +5	Pl +5
Mp +5	Ef +4	Pv +4
Mc +4	Eb +3	Pw +3
Xm	El +3	Pd +3
	Xe	Pc +3
		Xp

Many of these elements are under your control during and after your transition from the military. Those elements not under your control, are risk areas that must be analyzed, work arounds determined and should remain in focus.

MILITARY TRANSITION

The numbers represent your preparedness for transition within each element. As you successful evaluate each element with your current self-understanding, score yourself. A total score of 90 or higher is desired. Consult the chapter for each element to gain a full explanation and personal assessment assistance.

ACTIVITIES POST

TRANSFERABLE SKILLS	TOOLS	CIVILIAN NETWORK	DEVELOPMENT
Sc +5	Tr +5	Cp +5	Dm
Se +5	Tc +5	Cv +4	Dp
Sx +5	Ti +5	Cb +3	Dv
Xs	Tt +4	Cs +2	De
	T$ +3	Ct +2	Ds
	Xt	Xc	Xd

GR8TRANSITIONS4U

TOOLS

Tr	Resume
Tc	Cover Letter
Ti	Interview Prep
Tt	Interview Tips
T$	Total Compensation
Xt	Low Preperation

CIVILIAN NETWORK

Cp	Physical
Cv	Virtual
Cb	Branding
Cs	Shadow
Ct	Temping
Xc	Starting Late

POST-TRANSITION FACTOR

PROFESSIONAL DEVELOPMENT

Dm	Mentor
Dp	Path Analysis
Dv	Volunteer
De	Engage Management
Ds	Success
Xd	Failure to Develop

Let's Begin

You have made the right choice to start preparing for your transition. There is much to learn about yourself and the future you. So, let's begin to learn more about you.

Relevant questions are at the end of each section, constructed for your thought and activity.

- What are the risks of getting out?

- Are you uncomfortable with change?

- How will you embrace the change that is coming to your personal and professional life?

- What actions will you take to enable your successful transition?

- If you are intimidated, what are you going to do to reduce this emotion?

- Do your resume and professional networking profile correctly portray you and your desires?

Pre-Transition Factor

Market

U nderstanding the job market as it pertains to your personal situation is essential. Many change jobs multiple times after the military. Others find the right home immediately, due to either luck or more likely, careful planning. Instead of relying on luck, let us study some critical market elements and how they pertain to your transition.

1.1 Ma - Analysis

Trend analysis and knowing where the job market is going over the decade is extremely important. You do not want to get into a field that becomes obsolete after taking the time to perform the hard work required to become an expert. The Bureau of Labor and Statistics (BLS) has taken some of the guess work out of predicting the future. They have performed a study on the trends for the next 5-10 years for 100s of occupations.

US Bureau of Labor and Statistics Occupational Outlook:

www.bls.gov/ooh/

Similarly, if you are interested in learning what commercial industry says, check out the National Career Development Association (NCDA) at NCDA. org. Here you will find numerous articles on professional work environment, trends and direction.

> *I skate to where the puck is going to be, not to where it has been.*
>
> *~WAYNE GRETZKY*

Market sectors and jobs that are red hot now, may not be in a few years. So instead of trying to predict what will be hot in 10 years, you may need to take an attitude of continual reinvention, as the market trends shift.

The professional that stays current on the latest trends and jumps on the next wave of technological change are often rewarded handsomely. Remember, the best employees stay up to date on technology, are great communicators and radiate a personality of cooperation and congeniality.

Study the market trends and visualize how the trends are going to impact you, the field you are working in and your organization's capability. You will want to move with the trend through study and training, gaining early education and certification in the newly developing field. Try to work your way into a position where you can assist in implementing the new trend for your organization. In the meantime, vigilantly watch for the next trend.

Remain current and focused on the new trends within the market, working to reinvent yourself every few years. Skills change slowly. Knowledge becomes obsolete very rapidly. If you do not re-school and/or re-tool, you will find it difficult to remain viable, regardless of your chosen career field.

> *A knowledge worker becomes obsolescent if he or she does not go back to school every three or four years.*
>
> *~ PETER F. DRUCKER*

- Have you asked others how they reinvented themselves?
- What steps should you take, at this point during your transition?
- Have you looked at the next great trend or change in your chosen career field?

1.2 Mp - Your Personal Desires

Your new story is ready to be written as you begin your post-military career. During your transition from the military, it's important to take time to reflect on your personal desires and passions. As you dwell on your passion, think about your life's work, your calling or vocation. Fred Smith realized this when he studied delivery problems in Vietnam and created FEDEX after he got home from the war. More recently, Green Beret veteran Evan Hafer parlayed his passion for coffee and weapons as he formed Black Rifle Coffee Company, boldly stating in 2017 he would hire 10,000 veterans.

The good news is your previous experience will provide clues on your passion and perhaps your future occupation or vocation. Draw upon your knowledge from the military. What did you enjoy the most? Perhaps leading, mentoring of others, training, physical fitness, firing of weapons? These agreeable recollections will serve you well during your personal analysis and assist you in determining your professional direction.

By way of example, you may have found working in the arms room or organizing the supply room personally satisfying. If so, perhaps you are well suited for post-military career in logistics. Perhaps you found working with the personnel section on awards for your soldiers or initiating legal actions interesting. If so, you may look at getting a commercial Human Resources (HR) certification as you leave the service.

Your terrific recruiting skills could lead to a lucrative position in sales or business development. Or, perhaps the 18 months you spent as a schoolhouse instructor were personally satisfying. Because you enjoy instructing and enlightening others, you might consider being a corporate trainer or a high school educator. Have you been playing with computers at home, school or in the orderly room? Maybe now is the time to

Undecided about your next career field? Check out The Transitioning Combat Arms Professional!

study for the IT certification you have been thinking about. Discover commercial project management, especially if you enjoyed planning and executing field problems and operations. Perhaps you desire to attend seminary or go back to school.

Regardless, there are many options; with your fantastic path, stretched out in front of you! Now maybe the time to perform some analysis, figure out what you really enjoy doing and develop a path to success. Take time to consider how to evolve your passion into your next professional career.

There is no greater time to study your personal and professional desires, as they relate to your life's work or vocation. Accomplishing work you enjoy and are good at... will help the world the most. This is where your passions reside and what you were meant to do. Here you will find your life's work and this is exactly what the world needs you to do!

Bottom line, you owe it to yourself to think about what you are great at; because what you do uniquely well, is what you were meant to do. And, that is exactly what World War II Veteran Carl Buchan did, when he founded Lowe's. Foreseeing the dramatic increase in construction after World War II, Lowe's joint-owner Carl Buchan re-focused his brother's local company solely on home improvement products. He saw the gap in the market. After thinking about how he could personally influence the retail business, he helped propel Lowe's towards the current retail giant status.

- Have you taken time to consider where your passions lay?
- What do you enjoy doing?
- Do you have a plan to pursue your passion, even if you have to support yourself in some other method?

1.3 Mc - Company Selection

One thing is for sure. Finding a company that appreciates you will be invaluable. So how do you hedge your bet on your next employer?

When selecting your future company and armed with the right information, winning during your transition is not an impossible task. There is a way to hedge your bet when you are deciding on your future employer.

Fortune Magazine® has made corporate satisfaction research a much easier task by providing "The 100 Best Companies to Work For" at *www.fortune.com/best-companies/2021 search*. Based on a "Trust Index", this product is the most extensive workplace assessment in corporate America, with a random sampling of 230,000 people. Leadership, quality of life, professional satisfaction, benefits, hiring practices, recognition, training, and diversity programs are just a few of the surveyed areas.

Additionally, as a military member, you should look at Military Friendly's® "List of Best Military Employers' at *www.militaryfriendly.com/employers* and discern the best veteran friendly companies to seek. This website provides a list of over 100 companies perceived to have the best on-ramping, care and feeding of military veterans. From a military perspective, companies are evaluated in the areas of hiring, opportunity, advancement, culture, commitment, support, retention, and veteran policies.

So why not double down? If you have the option, why not pursue

Companies Making Fortune and Military Friendly Lists:

Accenture

Baird

Cisco

Comcast NBCUniversal

Deloitte

Farmers Insurance

Hilton

Northwell Health

Power Home Remodeling

Progressive Insurance

Quicken Loans

Stryker

Total Quality Logistics

USAA

Veterans United Home Loans

companies found on both lists during your job hunt? Interestingly, fifteen companies made both the Fortune List and the Military Friendly List in 2022. Here are a few with some of their most important attributes:

Cisco Systems – With over 171 work sites, CISCO rewards bright thinkers; where winners of its annual hackathon receive $25,000. The staff enjoys the freedom to innovate and make a meaningful difference through volunteering over 227,213 hours in 2016. Cisco was named Best of the Best by U.S. Veterans Magazine in 2016. They provide a VETS Employee Resource Organization, at all major U.S. sites, sponsors networking, mentoring, career development activities and information about how to get training in skills highly sought after by Cisco. Cisco has also pledged to train 1,000 veterans in cyber through the Joining Forces initiative, while creating a multimillion-dollar cyber scholarship program for veterans.

Veterans United Home Loans - Veterans United Home Loans is the nation's largest loan institution, specializing in helping veterans and service members obtain home loans backed by the Department of Veterans Affairs. This company both supports and hires veterans. They believe there is "no one better and more passionate about helping Veterans and service members secure the home of their dreams than those who served."

USAA - Headquartered in San Antonio with 87 work locations, this well-respected financial institution, combines meaningful work with serious benefits. Employees enjoy an 8% 401(k) match, six weeks of vacation, flexible schedule; with proud employees of the corporate mission and desire to assist the military. USAA has hired over 11,000 veterans and military spouses since 2006. USAA recognizes veterans are technical, agile, problem solvers, leaders, and loyal. Their approach to bringing them on board focuses on transition assistance, skills development, retention, sponsorship and veteran employee resource groups.

If you know "what" you want to do, why not start with a list of companies that are known to provide a higher quality of life?

I can think of no better way to prudently hedge your job hunt than starting your employment search with one of these companies listed by Fortune and/ or Military Friendly.

- Have you thought about your future company?

- What are some of the attributes that you desire in a company?

- Is it desirable for you to pursue a company when looking for your next position?

- Will finding the right work at the right location be satisfactory?

Your Environmental Factors

Environment

As you begin your transition it is important to understand the associated personal environmental factors. These factors affect you, your family, and your job opportunities. If you are like most, you will work after you transition from the military. If married, you certainly need to take into consideration your family's environmental requirements as you make decisions. Therefore, ensure you work through this section with them. If single, some of the considerations listed here may be relevant not only to you, but also to your extended family or your future family plans.

> *There are risks and costs to action. But they are far less than the long range risks of comfortable inaction.*
>
> ~ JOHN F. KENNEDY

Take your time and reflect on the following relevant sections and questions, using the information for your transition preparation. With the remote work environment becoming common place, ensure you have what you need to work from home, such as a quiet work place, computer, and internet.

2.1 │ Et │ - Timing

As the saying goes, "timing is everything." In any transition, timing is the key factor. Are you ready to leave the military? Do you have to leave the military? Are you satisfied with your military efforts and are ready to move on? These questions ascertain your level of readiness to transition from the service. With regard to your timing, this section includes an analysis of many elements, such as studying the educational benefits, developing and refining your resume, making interview preparations, and approaching certification. The following timing related topics are questions for your personal review and self-organization.

Is the Timing Right?

Are you ready to go? You do not want to regret your transition, as there is no going back if you still have something left to do in the military. There are many things to consider about timing. Gut instinct is probably not the best method for this determination. Looking at the associated timing issues and conducting self-assess-

> *The only reason for time is so that everything does not happen at once.*
>
> ~ ALBERT EINSTEIN

ments will likely provide a better result. These decisions should be made with a clear head and strong conviction. You may not be able to choose when to leave the service, but you can choose to prepare yourself as best as possible. The bottom line – prepare diligently with the limited time you have.

Are You Having Fun?

This may sound silly, but are you having fun in the military? Only you can determine if you are enjoying active duty. In general, the military lifestyle can be exciting with no two days being exactly the same. Many people look back at their time in service and remember their experience fondly. Others look back on their military service as an accumulation of tough days. However, you should expect to have tough days in your civilian job as well. Some will remark,

"Wow, did I do the right thing getting out?" Just remember, the grass is not always greener on the other side.

Have You Achieved Your Personal Goals for Military Service?

Achieving your personal goals in the military can be quite challenging, especially in today's world. You may have specific goals you were trying to obtain that are no longer attainable. You may also have a brilliant career ahead of you. Making the decision to get out of the service is always difficult. If you have accomplished your primary goals and objectives for military service, there is no need to fret about whether you should stay any longer. You may be painfully aware that you have obtained the highest rank possible. Remember, everyone gets passed over for promotion at some point. Congress continually adjusts the size of the military based on the needs of the nation and the defense budget. The services have had to reduce their end-strengths in the past, are doing it now, and will do so again.

Everyone undergoes assessment and some will be involuntarily released from active duty. If this is your situation, be prepared and transition in a positive manner. Remember, your time in the military denotes more Service to our nation than 93% of our fellow citizens. Thank you for your sacrifice.

Have You Found a Good Transitional Job?

Many veterans have stepped out of the Service straight into great jobs. This occurs with some degree of frequency, but it is not the norm. Often your first job is "transitional." For a variety of reasons, you may realize that your first job or company is no longer desirable. Remember, it is ok to test the waters when you first get out. Regardless, if you desire to grow and develop you may have to move on. Not everyone will have a job in his or her back pocket when transitioning. The question that you should ask yourself is "Am I taking all the appropriate steps to be ready for a job opportunity when it presents itself?"

- Have you accomplished all the goals you desired in the military?

- Do you already have a job lined up after the military? Is it solid?

- Do you have a backup plan?

- Have you performed the preparation necessary?

2.2 | Ef | - Family

As you transition, you need to consider your family needs. Being close to extended family may constrain your job searching to certain geographic areas. There are many family issues to consider during your transition. If there are special needs within your family, you may need to consider proximity to airports and hospitals. If you are a single parent, you will have to make these reflections yourself. Here are a few considerations.

Your employer should value families. Knowing how your employer values family life compared to your own desires, is worth considering. You can check this out by considering if they have family days or other events which can indicate how supportive the organization is to parents. You can read reviews of companies on job information sites like *Glassdoor* or *Indeed.* Is the company parent friendly? Is personal and family illness adequately supported?

Make sure your employer has family benefits and insurance coverage options if possible. Single member versus family coverage becomes important when a family is in consideration. Sometimes, smaller companies don't have the ability to cover the families with their employee health insurance. This may mean larger companies may be a better place to start if you are to be the primary source of insurance for your family or a single parent. Health care coverage pricing and benefit very greatly by company. Sticker shock of coverage

> *Family is a life jacket in the stormy sea of life.*
>
> ~ J.K. ROWLING

is common among transitioning service members. You can tell much about a company by how little or how much they pay into your health care plan.

Understand your prospective company's Paid-Time-Off (PTO) program or the equivalent of military leave. Understand sick leave, and Family Medical Leave Act (FMLA) policy and process for your future company. Taking care of kids is challenging during sickness and routine dental and orthodontics. Does your PTO "roll-over"? This is not the case everywhere. Unlike military leave, you may use or lose your PTO every year. Flexibility can be so important for families and knowing how to prepare can depend upon the employer's specific work policies. FMLA usually applies to companies of 50 employees and above and all government agencies which would include most school-based work.

Are there stipends or childcare options? How about a scholarship or family university credit? Are there typically after-work hours or shift work required? If you have family, you will need to check on these areas.

- Do you understand the impact on you and your family regarding the loss of military benefits?
- Does your spouse need or want to work?
- Can they find jobs at the location you desire?
- Will your spouse require more training or education?
- Will you or your family need to be near a university or college?
- Have you studied or discussed sharing your Post-9/11 G.I. Bill benefits with your family?

2.3 Eb - Financial Readiness

How is Your Financial Readiness? Do you have a financial plan? Have you saved enough money to survive the transition period? Is there more to it than just saving money? For many, the question is, "How much should you keep in a 'rainy-day' fund?" But is there more to the question?

There are a great many recommendations on this 'rainy-day' fund. According to the Bureau of Labor Statistics (BLS), an acceptable measure of three to six months' worth of expenses may no longer apply. Ryan Guiana, author of *The Military Wallet*, suggests shaping your emergency fund to equal three to six months of your monthly expenditures, not your salary. Further, your dollars need to be in short-term savings; not locked up in a retirement account – as you will want to avoid tax-related implications of early withdrawal.

If you are financially ready for your upcoming transition, you will have greater flexibility and more employment choices. You will have the ability to participate in training, relocation and other opportunities that will provide long lasting effects on your life. If you are unprepared financially, you limit your ability to respond to opportunities and put yourself and your family at economic risk due to employment gaps or other emergencies.

Why is financial readiness important to you? As a transitioning veteran, there are two fundamental reasons. The first is financial flexibility and the ability to navigate toward a preferred career path that maximizes lifetime earnings; versus taking the first job available. The second is to maximize your wealth, reduce any setbacks, and avoid financial hardships.

Realizing personal and professional opportunities beyond the military, including education, employment, entrepreneurship, volunteerism, additional public service, and travel reflect your personal financial preparation. Nearly half of veterans surveyed, state they had experienced financial challenges during their transition.

Develop and pursue the goal of financial flexibility as soon as possible. Further, consider saving beyond emergency savings to allow greater flexibility during transition. There are multiple strategies when financially preparing for transition. First, saving money is tried and true method.

> *No one has ever achieved financial fitness with a January resolution that's abandoned by February.*
>
> ~ SUZE ORMAN

Planning for your education and training is another. Treat your educational choices as a commodity – just like your savings, study closely the ROI for your educational choices. Use online tools and resources to assist with this endeavor.

Education and training assist in your transition by exposing you to capabilities, resources, and opportunities you missed because of time spent during military service. You are entering the workforce armed with robust educational benefits that enable both your hiring and advancement. Do not forget to analyze the implications of your spouse's employment status about your educational benefits such as the Post-9/11 G.I. Bill for scholarship or credentialing opportunities.

Study the benefits available to you - before, during and after your transition. Analyze the cost, time, and your personal responsibilities to obtain receive each benefit. Make sure to leverage free or low-cost training programs to receive industry recognized certifications and familiarize yourself with resources.

Additional great capabilities often overlooked are the Veteran and Military Service Organizations. These great outfits are full of concerned veterans that have come before you. They can provide invaluable information and access to free or low-cost programming. Also, make sure to talk with other veterans about their financial barriers encountered during transition and how they overcame them.

When considering employment options, think about long-term financial prospects versus short-term income gains. Understand you may need to use savings, as income will probably be reduced on occasion due to unemployment or underemployment, especially if you go the contractor route.

On a final note, if you should find the job search taking longer than expected, after departing the service, most states have provisions for you to draw unemployment or reemployment assistance benefits. Check with your state's workforce development website for more information.

- Do you understand how total compensation will impact your quality of life? (read T$ for more information on this subject)

- Have you given thought to what your "must have" salary will be? Is your expectation realistic? How do you know?

- Are you aware of the tremendous cost variation of health care plans in different organizations?

- Will you be able to align your educational opportunities, geographic location, and meaningful employment to maximize your financial readiness during transition?

- Are you pursuing opportunities to maximize lifetime earnings over short-term gains?

2.4 El - Location

During the recent pandemic, working location changed from a facility to home. A tremendous number of employees will now permanently work from home, but most will return to the office. Regardless, more than ninety percent of transitioning military personnel will move from their last duty station. Think carefully about your last move. Regulations change and each Service has different rules, but per the Defense Finance and Accounting Service (DFAS), military service members separating or retiring from active duty are entitled to reimbursement of relocation expenses. Therefore, you can save significant money if you have the military pay for the move to your desired location if it is closer than your home of record. Even then, you are only responsible for the difference financially.

Remember the saying "Location, Location, Location!" We are all quite familiar with this phrase. With the expense, you want to get it right the

> *"There is danger in thinking joy is a matter of location. If we can't find joy where we are, we probably won't find it anywhere."*
>
> ~ PHILLIP GULLEY

first time. It can be challenging and very costly to make a secondary move on your own dime. During your military transition, carefully study your future location. There are some particularly important factors to consider when selecting your separation or retirement location. Let us review some of the most important:

- **Job Environment** – This is probably the most critical element when selecting your separation destination or retirement location. There are a great many things to consider, many of which you may have already looked at. Have you studied the unemployment rate? Have you looked at the volume of defense contracts? How many civil servant or government related jobs exist in the local area? Many times, federal jobs require military skills. Are there veteran owned businesses in the area?

- **Physical Environment** – Let us consider the environment of the location that you are considering. Have you looked at the climate as it relates to your health, hobbies and personal activities? Some former military personnel have a need or desire to be near a military base so you can use the commissary, exchange and other facilities. Do you still desire the excitement of living overseas? Are you looking for a military friendly community? Do you prefer an urban or rural lifestyle? Often military service members need VA healthcare or other services from a VA hospital. Schools are always major considerations, such as specialty schools, quality and even the educational system. What about colleges and universities for yourself, spouse and kids? Finally, do you desire to live near extended family for their benefit?

- **Affordability** – We all need to be able to stretch a dollar. Some areas of the country have double the cost of living as others. Have you studied the cost of living in your desired area as compared to other regions of the country? Have you considered the cost of a home? Have you looked at state and local taxes? How about transportation costs? Is your military retirement pay going to be taxed?

Remember, you need careful consideration as it can be an expensive mistake to not consider all the factors when deciding upon your desired separation or retirement location.

- Do you need access to medical care or a Veterans Administration hospital?

- Are you looking for a rural or urban life experience?

- Is your work location near your interview site? Is it a long commute? Will you need to relocate?

- What is cost of living in your desired area as compared to other regions of the country?

- If you are looking at civil service, have you studied the locality pay for your desired region?

- What is the unemployment rate of your future location?

- How many government-related jobs exist in the local area?

- Do you want to live overseas? Have you researched and considered the challenges?

- Will your new employer help defer some of the associated relocation cost?

Personal Trait Awareness

Aristotle said, knowing who you are is key to success. Only through understanding your strengths and weaknesses can you be properly prepared for your transition. Work on shoring up your weaknesses and exploiting your strengths prior to your departure. But how do you properly prepare? Introspection will enable your ability to see the tremendous skills you obtained from the military. Let us look at some of these.

3.1 PI - Leader

There are many types and styles of leaders. Textbooks talk about autocratic, democratic, participative, laissez-faire and paternalistic leadership types and styles. You probably know where you fall out and can investigate these style types more if you desire. However, in a broad sense, there are really two career paths. The choice is yours – but you will likely have to choose between the two paths.

Technical Leader

Are you a technical leader or a people leader? One of the first professional questions many often ponder during military transition, is the decision of becoming a technical leader or a people leader. As compensation can often be similar, the question is a matter of personality and desire. You must know yourself, your capabilities and your inclination. However, there are several other considerations.

As a technical leader, you are a Subject Matter Expert (SME). For many, this is ultimately where their highest satisfaction is derived. You know a technology, a system, or a product better than anyone. You have years of experience, study and effort. You probably find it extremely rewarding to remain current and perform the hands-on work associated with being at the top of your technological field. As an expert, you know that technologies and paradigms change. Long-term technical leaders are experts, not in specifics but solutions.

One of the Greatest Challenges in Life is to Truly Know Yourself!

Great technical leaders often earn as much or more than managers. The technical leader that stays current on the latest trends and jumps on to the next wave of technological change is rewarded. To remain a viable technical leader, there are five steps that you must continually perform.

- Research (or better yet, create) the next hot IT movement or trend.

- Study the trend and visualize how it is going to change the field of IT and provide value to your organization's capability.

- Move professionally in the direction of the trend, through study and training.

- Gain early certification in the newly developing technological trend.

- Ensure you are at the helm during the organization's implementation of the new trend. As a valued technical leader, you have studied and know the new technology's capabilities better than anyone else in the organization.

Finally, the best technical leaders are communicators, cooperative and congenial. They share knowledge, inform, advise and educate others. This will not only provide recognition as the resident technical leader in that specialized function but increases your value as a mentor to the organization.

People Leader

Many consider people leaders as managers. People leaders emphasize coaching, developing, driving performance, inspiring and influencing. As a people leader, your major activity will be solving organizational challenges, not finding technical solutions. There are many things to consider when choosing to become a people leader.

As a people leader, you will invariably be pulled away from the keyboard and rely on technical leaders and their expertise. You naturally appreciate the challenges and abilities of your technical team. As a leader, you know your team, back them up and earn their trust while removing obstacles for team members. Never forget how to communicate with your technical leaders, and simultaneously learn to speak the language of corporate executives.

People leaders should have a certain mind set and demeanor, balancing the needs of the corporation and executives, with those of your peers and your technical team. When dealing with other departments, you should become a 'mediator' and 'facilitator' to gain consensus and approval. Being able to upward mentor, while keeping everyone synchronized and focused are key elements of people leadership.

Your Leadership Attributes are Desired by Civilian Employers!

At some point in your career in the commercial world, you will need to make a choice. Frequently, the technical/people leader decision is involuntary, but you can influence your own path. As you face this career question, determine if you desire to explore and pursue the leading edge of technology as a technical leader or be a people leader and climb the corporate ladder. Keep these concepts in mind as you continue your growth and professional development. Remember, know yourself and move to what you find enjoyable and rewarding, as this is where you will be most successful.

- Are you more comfortable leading people or working with technology?

- Do you desire to manage or remain highly skilled and technical?

- Can you do both, successfully?

3.2 Pv - Vocation

One of the many challenges that we face as we develop professionally is the vexing question of the pursuit of our dreams or paying the bills. Most of us are focused on enabling uninterrupted cash flow, the best company to pursue and what location to live. Many find an occupation that is in alignment with their immediate needs, in order to pay the bills. Reflection, analysis and alignment of fulfilling life work are pushed to another day, never unleashing your full personal passion.

Todd Henry explains in his book *Die Empty* that the graveyard is the most valuable land in the world as the buried lay with the unwritten novels, unlaunched businesses and all things that were to be accomplished tomorrow.

The bottom line, many of us have yet to discern the difference between our occupation and our vocation. The terms can be confusing. Merriam-Webster defines occupation as "the work that a person does, a job or an activity that a person spends time doing." On the other hand, vocation is defined as "a strong desire to spend your life doing a certain kind of work." In Latin, vocātiō means a calling or summons.

Trying to find contentment in your occupational task, will not be fulfilling your dreams and you will definitely become frustrated. It takes time and reflection to discern your life's work. However, once you know your vocation, pursue it. Until

> *"Our occupation is how we make a living...Our vocation, on the other hand, is what we're inherently wired for. It's less likely to consist of a set of tasks and more likely to consist of a set of themes."*
>
> ~ TODD HENRY,
>   THE ACCIDENTAL CREATIVE

the money starts to flow, your occupation may have to pay the bills to enable your continued vocational pursuit.

Reflect on what you value the most. You may treasure teaching, training, mentoring, cooking, building, helping others, spiritual growth, physical fitness or a multitude of other activities. Here you may find your passion and potential vocation.

Remain resolute in your pursuit of your life's work. A friend transitioned into a new job a few years ago, desiring to pursue his life's dream of becoming a stockbroker. After two years of studying, testing, licensing and working for a large brokerage house, introspection pushed him to pursue a different direction. He subsequently migrated to a consulting role where he coaches, enabling his desires and vocation through helping others.

Remember, your vocation is your life's work. It is what you were meant to do--and deep down inside, what you have always wanted to do. So take time out of your busy schedule for introspection and reflect upon your desires and talents. Tremendous satisfaction is found when making a living, pursuing your life's work.

- What did you enjoy the most from your military experience?

- Do you have a passion to learn something new?

- Has there been a time you desired to do "something" else? What was that "something"?

- Can you survive long enough financially to pursue your vocation?

3.3 Pw - Work-Life Balance

Work-Life Balance (WLB). You have worked hard in the military. Part of the assessment process is understanding where you reside on the WLB continuum. When looking for a job you should consider work-life attributes such as the demands that your occupation will require. Are you ready to climb the corporate ladder? You may find a demanding job and make a lot of money, but is that what you want for your post-retirement job? Occasionally, you can find a job with great WLB and make lots of money. However, if you make $120,000 you should generally expect to put forth a $120,000 effort.

A good WLB makes for better health and happiness. You can work hard and make a lot of money, but inadvertently affect your health and/or family life. Your personal investment in knowledge and experience will allow you to achieve greater expertise, accomplishment, fulfillment, and financial reward. However, it is easy to get caught up in a cycle of hard work and reward. Be cautious, as a successful career must have a balance or one will burn out personally, professionally, or both.

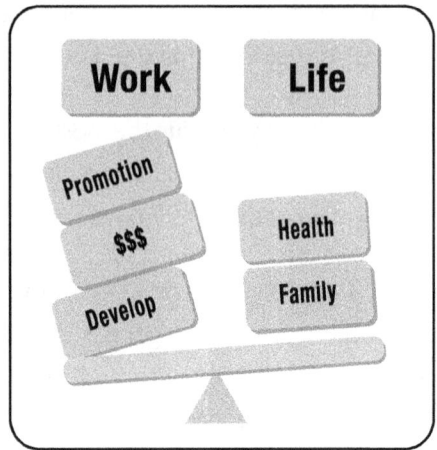

- How important are your leisure activities?
- Is your career the most important thing in life?
- Do you enjoy having opportunities to grow and relax with your family and friends?

3.4 Pd - Discipline

Many survive the military experience through strong faith, mental toughness, physical fitness and servant leadership. You brought some of these attributes with you to the military. Others were implanted by the service. Regardless, you own these attributes now.

Further, the military has shaped you through ingrained, service specific, core values. Civilians hear the words loyalty, duty, respect, selfless service, honor, integrity, and personal courage all the time. To you, they are much more than words. Each core value represents a tremendous personal quality. These values were engrained during your initial training and endure to this day. Further, your security clearance exemplifies your desire for a high quality, reliable and trustworthy lifestyle. You live

"If you want to change the world, start off by making your bed."

~ ADMIRAL WILLIAM H. MCRAVEN

these values every day, in everything you do, for the rest of your life.

Using these attributes and values, you have established a personal battle rhythm. You wake, you work out, and you eat right. You focus on the mission, your family, your subordinates and you use introspection to reflect upon your day's activities and your spiritual life. Bottom line, you may not do them in this order, but you get the job done and you have a personal method and rhythm.

On numerous occasions, you have heard, "If it ain't broke, don't fix it." You may be saying, "How does this relate to the section above?" Interestingly, when many military members begin to leave the service and transition into a different career, some of these phenomenal attributes get pushed to the wayside. Why do some veterans do this?

It is extremely important to establish and maintain your battle rhythm, utilizing those steadfast attributes you learned in the military during your transition and job hunt. Continue with your morning physical fitness routine, stay in shape, maintain your spiritual life, continue your professional development, stay engaged in family activities and focus on your job hunt.

These activities seem simple enough and there is no way you would intentionally do otherwise. However, there are so many distractors to take you away from your core attributes as you leave the service. There are a multitude of potholes you can fall into and quickly find yourself struggling in a strange new job market.

Therefore, if you have left any of these attributes behind, return to the basics. Apply what is ingrained in your military persona. Whatever schedule you have, whatever OPTEMPO you have, continue to maintain and develop the phenomenal habits ingrained during your military service.

Your core values are essential to your success. Employers find these core values highly desirable when looking for candidates to fill positions. They seek out military personnel for this reason. Therefore, these attributes make you highly marketable to employers. You own them, so use them to your advantage.

Years from now, you will reflect on these values and realize they not only sustained you, but also propelled you through life. Hold fast to the deep-rooted core values from your military service. They will not let you down.

- Have you performed a personal inventory?
- What issues are important to you?
- What are some non-negotiables?
- Do you need to "shape up" in any areas as you depart the service?
- Can you translate these values to your new resume and career?

3.5 Pc - Competitive Awareness

Have you taken time to analyze how well you know yourself with respect to your personal preparedness for transition and the marketplace? Are you ready? Have you studied the market you are interested in? How do you think you compare to peers within that market? Have you obtained the proper certification? There are many aspects to consider and you will make the transition easier if you are well organized and have some tools in your kitbag.

When evaluating solutions, you have used many great tools in the military such as the decision matrix and Course of Action (COA) analysis. A great tool for your transition preparation and enabling your ability to know yourself is the Strength, Weaknesses, Opportunities and Threats (SWOT) analysis

---

tool. SWOT analysis was originally developed for strategy development and is used extensively by business developers for determining competitive advantage in the marketplace. However, with a few minor modifications, you can use this tool to help determine your personal competitive capability within the marketplace during your military transition. SWOT analysis forces you to think about the external factors regarding your future career while providing direction on those areas for change. Performing a self-analysis to determine your abilities and shortcomings using SWOT will not only give you a greater understanding of yourself but will also provide a level of confidence needed for a competitive edge.

Competition is always a good thing. It forces us to do our best.

~ NANCY PEARCY

Think about and ask yourself questions within each quadrant to begin the analysis. To provide initial thoughts on the type of questions you should be asking yourself, a sample SWOT Analysis is provided….. but you need to perform your own.

The SWOT diagram below provides inquisitive attribute statements, common to military personnel in transition, based on typical experience. Study each statement within each quadrant. Determine if you have an advantage or if you need some work in that area. Think of additional questions to ask yourself within each quadrant to enhance the self-analysis. Use the results of your personal SWOT analysis to determine how well you stack up against your competitors and what areas you should seek improvement.

Strengths	Weaknesses
Internal, positive aspects under your control to exploit:	*Negative aspects you control and can improve upon:*
Security Clearance	Lack of commercial work experience
Military work experience	Lack of understanding of job market
Education	Lack of commercial vernacular
Technical knowledge	Negative self-image
Transferable characteristics such as - communications, leadership, teamwork ability to work under pressure, work ethic, etc.	Dealing with negative misconceptions about military service members
Innate Military Core Values	Not understanding how to become marketable
Ability to assess and perform introspection on capabilities	Lack of commercial experience or career knowledge
Ability to gain certification	

Opportunities	Threats
Positive, external conditions outside of your control that you can exploit:	*Negative, external conditions you cannot control, but can reduce the effect:*
Career field growth	Knowing your competition
Military friendly companies	Negative misconceptions about former military
Opportunities available through further educational and certification	Competitors with better job hunting capabilities
Funding of school through GI Bill program	Obstacles - lack of education and/or certification
Fields in need of military attributes	Competitors with superior skills)
Opportunities available with greater preparation and self-knowledge	Failure to stay marketable
Opportunities by greater understanding of commercial career field and market place	
Networking with seasoned Professionals	

- Have you taken time to think about your personal strengths and weaknesses?

- Have you listed out the opportunities that are in your future?

- Are you focusing on the issues that you can control?

- Have you considered your way ahead, personally configuring for those areas that you cannot control?

- Have you closely reviewed the competition?

- Is your security clearance a strength for your transitional job?

4.0

Transferable Skills

Your skills are transferable. Can you incorporate them into your military transition to acquire a position in your desired career field? Business author Peter Drucker believed workers must go back to school every 3-4 years. You can quickly become obsolete if you do not pursue something viable with regularity. How do we use and enhance our transferable skills?

The challenge is getting cross trained, enabling you to compete in the commercial market. Understanding commercial concepts and terminology is the first step in cross training. Performing this type of study will assist you in certification, increase your confidence, enabling you to apply and interview.

4.1 Sc - Certification

Your personal reinvention can be obtained through training, education and/or certification. Training refers to the act of instilling skills through determined instruction. Education provides theoretical knowledge. Either may be obtained on your own or in a classroom or institution.

Certification must be conferred by a certifying organization. Certification is a method to prove to the world, your mastery of a body of knowledge. The certifying body assures the certified individual has the qualifications necessary to perform a job or task.

Interestingly, there is a significant variety in licensing and certifications. Some certifications follow hot new technologies and trends. Others have become standards in the workplace. A sure-fire way to stimulate your career is to obtain certification, making you marketable within a workforce sector. Understanding how to focus on the right certification to improve your strengths will provide dramatic professional growth. To that end, let us look at a few certification types.

Entry Level Certifications

If you lack education, certification can become a great equalizer when seeking a new career. When transitioning from military, entry level certifications allow examination with little experience. They are usually generalized across multiple career fields and the cost is reasonable. Entry level exams cover terminology, basic knowledge, and certify the ability to understand concepts learned. Using IT as an example, some certifications cross multiple career fields and is a great way to start. Broad-based certifications will pay dividends by enabling you to compete for multiple entry level IT positions and by providing better personal ROI. Some certifying organizations such as CompTIA®, specialize in providing credentials for boosting the initial performance of IT professionals across multiple IT fields. As referenced in The Transitioning Military IT Professional, entry level certifications are designed to assist those entering the field by providing quality certifications that are recognized by hiring officials and employers. In addition to being commonly recognized in commercial industry, many CompTIA exams meet Department of Defense (DoD) Directive 8570.01-M requirements, which are essential if you desire to work in IT as a defense contractor.

Numerous certifications for logistical and mechanical skills, such as the renowned Airframe and Powerplant License (A&P) are required for securing a position within commercial industry. This license requires 18 months of practical experience with either power plants or airframes, or 30 months of practical experience working on both at the same time. As an alternative to this experience requirement, you can graduate from an FAA approved aviation maintenance technician school. You must pass a written examination, an oral test, plus a practical test.

Advanced Certification

Advanced and more specific certifications are essential as you mature and grow within your career field. Why? Regardless of your stated knowledge, nearly all managers regard certifications as an effective measurement to judge your value

> *Attitude, performance, commitment to team - these and a certificate make you certified.*

to the organization. Therefore, they look for the appropriate certification on resumes. Many hiring managers believe certification distinguishes a dedicated individual and ensures the right person is on the job. Further, many believe a quality work culture is created by hiring certified candidates, which enables the organization to be more competitive for the customer. Therefore, as you transition from the military, it is in your best interest to certify early and remain current in your chosen field.

Typically, advanced certifications are higher in cost and might require another certification as a pre-requisite. Many advanced certifications are experienced based, meaning that you will have to demonstrate 'seat time' before you can even apply. You will need to prove comprehension, application, and analysis on these exams, as the scenarios presented test your experience.

Management Certifications

If you are seeking a management track, get project or program management certified, quickly. The Project Management Institute® (PMI) offers many certifications, but there are over 750K active Project Management Professional® (PMP) certified managers world-wide. Therefore, if the job announcement requires or desires the PMP, your job search will be challenging if you are not certified. If you are planning on obtaining the PMP, do it quickly. History dictates that the exam will change, corresponding with the next release of the *Project Management Body of Knowledge® (PMBOK)*. Check out *The Transitioning Military Project Manager* and *The Transitioning Military Logistician* for more on many certifications.

Professional Certifications

There are specific career field certifications, such as the Professional in Human Resources® (PHR) for Human Resource Specialists. Many other career fields offer certification as well, such as the Certified Professional Contracts Manager® (CPCM), offered by the National Contract Management Association (NCMA). If you are still on active duty, *The Transitioning Combat Arms Professional* suggests obtaining Defense Acquisition Workforce Improvement Act (DAWIA) certification from the Defense Acquisition University (DAU) before you transition. It is free for DoD employees and is widely recognized by employers within the defense contracting environment. For a comprehensive look at other career field certifications check out.

- Do you need a certification?

- Does your chosen career field require it?

- Have you started preparing for your certification?

- Does your desired certification require experience? Do you have the experience necessary for the certification?

4.2 Se - Education

According to the BLS, the average earnings for workers without a high school education is less than $600 a week. A Bachelor of Science (BS) is more than double and a professional degree will bring you on average over $1800. You either apply the effort to get a degree, or on average, you are going to work harder and longer. No matter which route you select, if you did not get your degree before or in the service, now may be the time to do it. Your post 911 G.I. Bill can be used and it is available to you as a valuable tool.

In some ways, this may be the most valuable military Service benefit you obtain. It is essential that you use this to your advantage and figure out how to develop those areas you were most interested in because that is where your passions lie.

And where your passions lie is where you will be doing your best work. There is a path to using the Post 9/11 G.I. Bill and these steps should point you in the right direction.

First, choose a program and school that aligns with your goals and apply for admission. You can continue to complete the steps below before you have received an admissions decision.

Second, obtain the "golden ticket." To do this, you need to submit the Veteran Affairs (VA) application for the Post-9/11 G.I., AKA VA 22-1990 form, through www.vets.gov. The online application can also be accessed

Post 9/11 G.I. Bill

www.vets.gov

from, www.ebenefits.va.gov. After this is complete, the VA will send a Certificate of Eligibility or the "Golden Ticket" by mail. You may also download a copy from either of these sites once available.

Third, submit a copy of the Certificate of Eligibility to the admissions office and the school's veteran's office. Many of the college or university veteran's offices will assist you with the procedures if you are having issues.

Even though you will receive a stipend and have much of your schooling paid for, make sure to apply for Federal Financial Aid. The Free Application for Federal Student Aid (FAFSA) found at www.studentaid.gov/h/apply-for-aid/fafsa is a form completed by college students to determine their eligibility for student financial aid. Understand that FAFSA veteran education benefits are available in addition to what is offered via G.I. Bill Benefits. Not all types of financial aid for veterans via FAFSA are need-based. Therefore, everyone should apply. The G.I. Bill is not your only college payment option. Veterans often do not know or forget this. Many have long-term educational plans that are not fully covered by the GI Bill and knowledge of options is essential.

Start early and leverage your educational opportunities while on active duty. Plan for a longer and potentially more expensive transition than you anticipated. Consider the ability to complete degree requirements or credit transfers should you relocate, to maximize your G.I. Bill benefit.

- Have you acquired the "golden ticket"?

- Have you selected and applied to a college program or school?

- Can you accomplish these tasks prior to your departure from the military?

4.3 | Sx | - Experience & Skills Transfer

You may be unaware of the significance of your traditional military skills such as professionalism, confidence, positive attitude, communications and organizational skills. These are all highly desired by commercial companies.

Many of these characteristics are crucial attributes for managers in commercial settings. The following soft-skills are ingrained in service members and are highly "resumeable." In other words, with the correct wording, there may be a place on your resume for these skills.

You are **performance oriented** –As a service member; lives depend on you. The outcomes are unwavering. You understand the challenge, therefore you get the job done.

You have been in the combat zone; you have learned how to stay calm and function under extreme pressures. **Grace under fire** is second nature to you –This skill will make some personnel and management calamities look trivial.

Effective communicators build teams. Teams accomplish goals and you know how to lead a team. You understand team dynamics and their importance, enabling you to communicate and motivate.

Your experiential **leadership** lessons as a Noncommissioned Officer In Charge (NCOIC), platoon leader and, team leader, enable you to work in a hierarchical

---

team-oriented environment. You know how to take orders. You also know how and when to give them.

You are **self-aware** and practice **self-sacrifice.** As a military leader, you watch out for your team first, often sacrificing and denying yourself. Servant-leadership is a popular term in the commercial world today. However, it is not always encountered in the Fortune 500.

You need to know how to describe and apply these skills to your resume. Further, you will want to discuss how your personal skills and capabilities will provide value to the interviewing organization. Take time to practice interviewing, so that you can relay and finesse the appropriate personal response to the questions future employers will ask.

Finally, your leadership and management skills are invaluable. If you enjoy managing and leading teams, your skills as an action officer, training officer, operations planner, commander, platoon sergeant, are all military terms that equate to project manager in the civilian world. Regardless of your service background, as a military leader, you already perform many project management functions daily. You are probably just unaware of how closely it relates to your military leadership and management work. Your skills may be a perfect fit for the project management career field. You can read more about this in *The Transitioning Military Project Manager.*

- Have you thought about applying your traditional military skills to your resume?

- Have you reflected on your soft skills and know how to introduce them in an interview?

- Could your leadership and/or management skills put you on a project management career path?

5.0

Tools for the Kit Bag

A powerful, impactful, well-written resume using commercial and business language, combined with the right format and branding power, can set you apart and propel you to a rewarding position in the private sector. Your resume and cover letters are your personal calling cards. Additionally, knowing how to interview is an essential skill not often taught. Let us look at your preparation for these essential tools.

5.1 Tr - Resume

Your military experience is unique! Many transitioning service members have challenges talking about the uniqueness of their military experience with the hiring managers. You must capitalize on the extraordinary capabilities that you have achieved while in the Service. You will need to speak to the value and difference you made while serving in each position. Capture the size of the effort, quantity of personnel, and if applicable the multiple geographic locations that you had to coordinate with and/or synchronize associated with each position. You will need to talk about the impact and volume of what you routinely handled.

There is a definite skill in writing a resume. It is an art to speak about yourself and connect your value to the value desired by a company. It is a science to include the key terms in your resume so a computerized search engine can identify those words within your resume and put it at the top of their pile for consideration. There are many tools and books to assist you with this.

To create a well branded and powerful resume you will need to go beyond providing your job description. You will most likely need to write and re-write your resume multiple times. Be smart with your network; use military friends and colleagues who have transitioned well into civil servant positions. Use other networking groups from professional or other non-military organizations for commercial insight and guidance. You will need to modify the resume until you are comfortable with it. If you are challenged with resume writing and have money for professional preparation, this may be a good investment.

It is recommended that you post your resume on hiring sites like Monster.com, Indeed.com, and CareerBuilder.com. These sites are scanned on a regular basis and you will get frequent emails informing you of potential opportunities. Even if the job is not exactly what you desire, apply! In

Gr8 Place to Translate Military Skills:

military.com/veteran-jobs/skills-translator

addition to potentially gaining a greater appreciation for the company and associated career opportunities, the interview experience is unbelievably valuable.

When your resume gets in front of a recruiter or hiring manager, it has approximately twelve seconds to do its job. It needs to be clear, error-free and most importantly, show your value! Remember to be bold. Most of us have a sense of humility, but a resume is not the place to be humble.

A chronological resume lists your work history in reverse chronological order – with the current, or most recent job, first. Employers typically prefer chronological, as it is easy to see which jobs you held and when you worked. This works well for job seekers with strong, solid work history.

Use a functional resume to focus on your skills and experience, rather than on your chronological work history. This resume is used most often for changing careers or gaps in employment history.

A combination (hybrid) resume lists your skills and experience first. Your employment history is listed next. This resume highlights your relevant skills to the job you are applying for, while providing chronological work history that employers prefer.

Employers tend to favor a resume that is easy to follow and clearly communicates your professional track. If you plan on writing your own and have 10 or more years of experience and education, select a format that concentrates on your assignments, your accomplishments (value), and education. A great guide for specific resume examples and templates can be found in "The Military to Civilian Transition Guide: Secrets to Finding Great Jobs and Employers."

Also, be aware that commercial and civil service resumes can be quite different. A few years ago, it was best practice to create a special resume with a specific format when applying for civil service positions, such as month with your dates and contact information for your supervisors.

- Have you put together a draft resume?

- Has anyone in your desired career field, outside the military, reviewed your resume?

- Do you know any human resource or staffing representatives that can look at your resume?

5.2 | Tc | - Cover Letter

Veterans often fret over their resumes, spending hours translating military skills, seeking advice and tailoring for a specific job. Significant mental energy is dedicated to this critical job seeking essential. However, when it comes to the on-line application, often exhaustion sets in and there is little energy left for their meager and neglected cover letter.

When pondering the cover letter question, you may contemplate the following:

- Do I really need a cover letter?

- Is anyone going to read this?

- Should I just use a generic cover letter format and get this task over with?

- With my relevant information in the resume, do I need to spend much time on this?

Experts in the staffing field say that a well-written cover letter, not a resume, will land you more job interviews. As a transitioning service member, it would be a tragic mistake not to spend the time and effort necessary for a personalized cover letter, each time you apply. Here are a few pointers:

Be brief. Do not overdo your letter. A short, pithy, excited and to the point cover letter will get read. Human Resource (HR) folks are not going to read through a long boring document when they are quickly scanning for the right candidate. Often, less is more.

The layout is important. Address your cover letter to someone. Find out who will receive the cover letter and address your cover letter to them. If you cannot get this information, open with a subject line with something like: "Cover Letter: Your Name, Your Credential." Remember, "Dear HR Team Member" is lame.

Try to open the letter with a hook. The first sentence must grip the reader. The hook will almost guarantee your cover letter and resume get a much closer look. You can do this through one of several methods.

- You can express your excitement for the job opportunity. This translates to motivation and dedication. This can make HR want to find out more about your qualifications.

- Use Keywords - Knowing that scanning or applicant tracking systems are widely used, another approach to the opening line is to make it keyword-heavy.

- Do not be afraid to use names or a connection. This is a foreign concept to many service members because we do not do this in the military. If someone in your professional network refers you, do not hesitate to drop the name, straight away. This is done all the time in the civilian world and people often receive referral dollars for doing so. Remember, time is money and this method helps HR rapidly fill positions with quality candidates.

- Your opener can impact employers by demonstrating your knowledge of recent news associated with the company. Associate the knowledge to the position in which you are applying. Let them know why you would be the best candidate as relative to this news.

Make sure your cover letter communicates what you can do for the business, how you will benefit the company and its bottom line. You may need to take a few minutes and perform some internet searches to relate your added value in clear terms.

> *There is only one purpose of the cover letter; get job interviews.*

Ensure you have an enthusiastic ending and request something. Ask the employer for some kind of action. Go ahead and request an opportunity to interview this week or earliest convenience. You do not get what you don't ask for. This is often a great way to end your cover letter. Thank them for the opportunity. Your closing should assume you are going to land the interview.

You want to be able to rapidly reuse your cover letter repeatedly. You need to create a folder for cover letters. This will enable you to quickly tailor the opening and cover letter to relate your skills to the essential elements of the job announcement. Do not forget to save your cover letter for quick modification and future use.

Remember, the cover letter is your marketing sheet.

- Have you put together a cover letter?
- Are your transitioning peers using cover letters?
- Does your cover letter reflect your personality?

5.3 | Ti | - Interview Preparation

Let us talk about three essential functions you should accomplish prior to any interview: research, review and rehearse.

Research!

Understanding your potential new organization prior to the interview is essential. In addition to the size, location and history, you'll want to know some details about your future employer. You'll want to research the company strengths and know the differentiators for this company? What makes it better than its competitors? Learn what you can from the corporate website. A good place to start is the "About Us" section. Having this knowledge will allow you to engage in confident discussion.

Research the company's financials. This can be found in the investor relations tab on their website. Or if traded publicly, you can find basic investor information by looking at the company's financial statement on Google. Google automatically provides a summary of the company, financial analysis, latest news, performance and competitors. Seek out information on new products and services, financial challenges and future market positioning. Make sure you understand the market as it relates to the company and the converse.

Look at social media and see what is being broadcast on LinkedIn, Facebook, Twitter, and corporate blogs. Does the company respond to social media concerns/reviews? Are there a lot of complaints by employees? Understanding the corporate culture is essential to find if the company is a good place for you to fit in. Far better to know in advance, rather than realizing later you were not a good match.

Finally, if you know the names of the individuals conducting the interview, research them. Check them out on social media. Learn about their "likes" and if they have any pet peeves. Do you know folks that are connected to them? If so, can you get in touch? The more you know about the interviewer, the more likely you will have a successful first engagement with them. Rest assured; they are checking you out on social media prior to your arrival.

Review You!

Make sure your resume is in great shape. Are there items to update now that you have performed company research? Refine your resume for any mistakes or differentiating features. As always, be prepared to provide several copies of your updated resume.

Do you have copies of your certifications, diplomas, transcripts and licenses? Is your suit in good shape? Do you need new shoes or a belt? Does your shirt look tired, even though it is pressed?

Do you know the exact location of the interview? Have you been to this location before? Do you know where to park? Will parking or driving become a potential challenge to your arrival time? Do you need to perform a map or physical reconnaissance? Far better to know these answers in advance.

Rehearse!

This final "R" is essential. If you have not interviewed in a while, read up on the process. Find a location away from home to practice. If you find it difficult getting into a rehearsal mindset, put on your suit. Not only will this give you the right attitude, but it will also allow you to test your clothing for comfort, fit and completeness.

Job interviews are like first dates. First impressions count and outcomes are unpredictable.

You need to find a friend, spouse or coworker for interview rehearsal. If you are forced to rehearse alone, practice out loud. If possible, record and replay your answers. Determine what sounds good and what needs improvement.

Think about what kind of questions you are going to be asked, relative to the position. There are numerous common interview questions online for rehearsal. Behavioral interview questions are quite common, where you are asked to discuss a personal experience relative to the job. Sometimes you will be asked puzzling questions, such as "How many basketballs would it take to fill the room?" For these, they will be more interested in your method, than your answer.

You may experience many types of interviews. You are often subject to a phone or Skype session prior to a face-to-face interview. An interview can become an all-day affair, including lunch or dinner. Be aware, they will be watching every move to determine if you are a good fit, organizationally.

With preparation using the three "Rs" you will be confident for your interview. Remember, confidence is the expectation of a positive outcome and it is contagious.

The more interviews you attend, the wider range of opportunities you will receive. Remember, applying and interviewing for jobs is a career long process and it takes lots of practice.

- Have you looked closely at the company you are interviewing? Are you a good fit?

- If you are driving to the interview, do you know the route, ETA, parking, entrance locations of the sites?

- Do you have a good-looking suit?

- Can you ask HR or recruiter how to dress for that company?

- Are you planning on taking copies of your reviewed resume, certifications, and education with you?

5.4 Tt - Interview Tips

As a transitioning service member, many of your military attributes such as work ethic, leadership and punctuality are in high demand by civilian corporations. You are a desirable candidate. However, you do not want to be perceived as "too military" by the interviewer.

By way of example, military customs and courtesies show respect and reflect self-discipline. You spent months learning how to stand properly for the military. Chapter 4-16 from Army "Soldier's Guide", states "When speaking to or being addressed by a noncommissioned officer of superior rank, stand at parade rest until ordered otherwise." These are great habits, but they have no place in the civilian job interview.

The problem is attention and parade rest will scare or confuse the civilian interview panel. You may be the most qualified person they interview and get screened out because you are perceived as "too military." While thinking that you are rendering an appropriate level of courtesy, you may be frustrating your job prospect. Your interviewer(s) may not just be confused, they could be alarmed. Old habits are hard to break, so let's run down a few Do's and Don'ts for your first civilian interview.

Try to avoid any jargon. Don't use words like "Top", "Helos", "29 Palms" or the "Big Sandbox." Similarly, do not use nomenclature or unit names. These will not be understood. Depending on what part of the country you are from and where you are interviewing, repeatedly addressing the interviewer or members of the panel as "sir" or "ma'am" could be cause for concern.

Leave your uniform at home; any part of it. Believe it or not, your dress uniform "Corfam" shoes are not in order. Get yourself an entire civilian suit, including shoes, socks and a dress belt.

Don't be rigid! Again, you do not want to come off as "too military." On the other hand, don't get too comfortable! And of course, no cursing!

What should you do? If you are just getting out, meet up with other veterans that have transitioned and talk about the interview process. Before the interview, try to gain as much intelligence about the company as you can. Reach out to your social network and find out what the culture is like. If you know who will be conducting the interview, try to gain some insight into them and the position.

Have some specific examples of previous work and leadership experiences that were particularly challenging and how you overcame the problem. You will be asked behavioral or situational interview questions and you need to be ready.

Thoroughly answer questions, demonstrating your personal and professional growth, without throwing anyone under the bus.

Make sure you have some questions for the interview panel. We do not often ask a lot of questions in the military, but this is the time and place to show that you have researched the company and are interested in the job and the team you are joining.

Bring your highly desirable military attributes to the interview, but don't be perceived as overly military! Finally, be yourself and don't be afraid to toot your horn!

- Have you invested in an appropriate interview close?
- Have you researched the company you are interviewing with? Do you know their locations and their annual revenue?
- Do you know what department the position you are interviewing is located?
- Did you search the internet for leaders, managers, work within the department?

5.5 T$ - Total Compensation

You have enjoyed great benefits on active duty. Some civilian companies offer great benefits; others do not! Talk to anyone that has been out for a while and they will tell you there is a significant variation between companies for benefits such as PTO and insurance.

After the initial offer, 60% of American workers take the salary proposed and accept the job, not closely examining the benefits and total compensation. Understand the total offer as it relates to your personal circumstances. Ask your future employer lots of questions. If they get irritated or elusive and the salary is low and non-negotiable, maybe the job is not the right fit. The best offense is the superb defense. Be prepared with the knowledge to know what the fair and equitable salary would be for you. Remember, you may not have the opportunity to renegotiate for at least a year.

How do you prepare for salary and benefit negotiations? You should find all the benchmark salary information available for the position you are applying for and arm yourself. You will need to spend adequate time conducting research on average salary ranges for similar jobs in the industry and your local area. Check out websites like Payscale.com, Salary.com or Glassdoor.com.

Decide on an appropriate salary range for yourself. Research and calculate your appropriate salary based on the research that you have conducted and then your personal situation. It is also good practice to identify your "must have" point.

Your "must have" point is the amount you must have to even consider the job. Think about the reasons why you would not be willing to accept a lower amount. If you provide personal reasons such as "both kids are in college," expect push-back. You will need data based on your special qualifications and experience.

A better approach is understanding the total compensation package. This means to look at benefits such as bonuses, medical, dental, education, and 401K match. If a bonus is part of the package, make sure you have the program in writing and understand exactly how the bonus program works. Further, if PTO is important to you and the company is rigid about the number of days or hours off, ask if you can buy more. Look at the total cost of your medical, dental, short-term and long-term disability insurance. How much life insurance will you need? Can you buy more? Is the insurance a good value compared to your other life insurance policy? All these total compensation elements are essential to review. Don't forget to study the location for tax, commuting, parking, housing, crime and schools.

You are in control and only you will accept the offer. There are areas of the offer you can negotiate and other areas you cannot. Study the benefits and consider how to negotiate. Always ask for time to provide an answer. When it comes to understanding total compensation, most look at three components: direct financial compensation, indirect financial compensation, and non-financial compensation. Also, there are personal quality of life issues to consider.

Here are a couple of real-world examples.

SCENARIO 1:

After leaving active duty and joining the reserves, John took a huge pay cut and went to work for another company. People thought he was crazy. Turns out he was crazy like a fox. The new job was close to home. He saved 50 miles a day on his vehicle, reducing tolls, fuel, maintenance costs, while recovering 75 minutes a day from his commute. His dental coverage for his son's braces was running out just before his job transition. With the new job, he received a new dental plan, which paid the remaining 2-year orthodontic bill. His educational benefits and 401k were both better. Finally, within two years he was making the same salary as before and his total compensation was much higher.

SCENARIO 2:

Mike took a well-paying defense contractor position in a nearby state. He received a $42K uplift in wages over his military pay and a $5k sign on bonus which he used toward the move. But his new company's medical insurance was very expensive, and the deductibles were high. Accustomed to paying neither city nor state tax; Mike was simultaneously being forced into a higher federal tax bracket. Housing was more expensive; his commute was 50 minutes longer each day and he had to pay to park. Bottom line, with the very nice salary bump, he thought he was making a lucrative financial move for his family. He was wrong!

These accounts are based on real events. As you look at the job offer, closely review the total compensation. If you are being given an excellent offer for your personal situation, then skip the negotiation and take the offer. However, if you want the job and the offer seems low, based on your research, don't be intimidated. Remember, salary and benefits can be negotiated with a little personal finesse. Be assured, you are highly desirable. Employers want you! Take some time for research and you will make a great choice for your family as you transition from the military.

- Do you understand how total compensation will impact your quality of life?

- Have you given thought to what your "must have" salary should be?

- Are there some benefits you cannot live without, like health care?

- Is your work location near your interview site? Is it a long commute?

6.0

Civilian Network

S   Some estimate that up to 70% of all jobs are not published on publicly available job search sites. Further, research shows that 60% or more jobs are filled through networking. All the veterans in the book *The Transitioned Veteran*, from the *Transition Military Book Series* cited networking as one of their top 3 tasks to work on during transition.

Developing your network is a multifaceted task. You must have a local network and a virtual network. If you are moving, you should develop a network at your new location, early if possible. In this section you will learn of the importance of networking, branding, developing a job shadowing experience and temping. All these elements may play an essential role in your transitional success.

6.1 Cp - Physical

As mentioned above, this essential element is one part of building a network. A great way to develop local or physical networks is to volunteer at your local military association such as the Navy League, Association of the United States Army (AUSA), or Armed Forces Communications and Electronics Association (AFCEA). However, getting off the installation and meeting with local organizations is a better way to expand your network.

Perhaps you could join your local Toastmasters Club, which can build your network, develop potential lifelong friends, and learn to speak in public with

---

greater ease and finesse. The Tampa Bay Area has over 51 Toastmasters Clubs. The Project Management Institute has chapters in over 110 cities in the United States and 237 chapters around the world. Additionally, there are numerous other professional organizations that you can get involved with around the country and potentially in your local area.

These organizations and associations will not only offer national meetings, but often conduct regional and local chapter meetings. Each one of these groups actively seeks volunteers. Volunteer and you will not only grow in your understanding of the commercial professions and enhance professional skills; you will also actively increase your network. Some of these organizations offer certifications, and as previously discussed can provide vital assistance in getting in the door for an interview.

Networking allows you to become a known commodity while building meaningful relationships. You will meet and exchange information which will invariably help you while helping others. Through these relationships, you establish trust and increase your interpersonal confidence, while building your professional credibility and enabling personal opportunity.

By way of example, PMI is one of these professional networking organizations, promoting the professional development of project management professionals in the commercial environment. PMI supports the profession by providing a community of practice where members network and improve their professional skills. Today, thanks to the assistance of Gr8Transitions4U and others, PMI® now offers military liaisons at most local chapters to assist you during your transition.

Organization	URL
Agile Alliance	www.agilealliance.org
APICS - supply chain and operations management	www.apics.org
Association for Computing Machinery (ACM)	www.acm.org
Association of Information Technology Professionals (AITP)	www.rtp-aitp.org
Association of Shareware Professionals (ASP)	www.asp-software.org
Computer Professionals for Social Responsibility (CPSR)	www.cpsr.org
Council of Supply Chain Management Professionals	www.cscmp.org
Independent Computer Consultants Association (ICCA)	www.icca.org
Institute for Supply Management – ISM	www.ism.ws
Institute of Electrical and Electronics Engineers (IEEE) Computer Society	www.computer.org
International Association of Public Health Logisticians (IAPHL)	www.IAPHL.org
International Society of Logistics – SOLE	www.sole.org
Association for Women in Computing	www.awc-hq.org
Network Professional Association (NPA)	www.npanet.org
Optimist International	www.optimist.org
Project Management Institute (PMI) ®	www.pmi.org
Rotary International	www.rotary.org
Scrum Alliance	www.scrumalliance.org
Society for Human Resource Management (SHRM)	www.shrm.org
Software Development Forum (SDF)	www.sdforum.org
The Academy of International Business	www.aib.msu.edu
Toastmasters	www.toastmasters.org
Warehouse Education and Research Council	www.werc.org

6.2 Cv - Virtual

The virtues of a virtual network cannot be underestimated. You cannot really put a price tag on the "special person" that helps you find a job. In this networked age, the "special person" is not necessarily someone you have ever met.

Most military members are reluctant to build a LinkedIn® account. That is understandable! Operational security is a daily consideration during your military Service. Social media, including professional or business oriented social networking, is often frowned upon. But as you begin your transitional journey, know that a LinkedIn profile is essential to your job search and is serious business. Further, professional networking is a critical tool when you desire to develop connections and build a powerful virtual network.

The first step is to create a quality professional profile if you have not done so already. You need a professional looking photograph, sans uniform. You want to optimize your profile so that you stand out, making sure it depicts who you are and what you want to do. You do not want to have a resume or LinkedIn profile that says "Jack-of-All-Trades". Translate your previous positions into civilian terms, knowledge gained by studying professionals in your career field on LinkedIn. Like your resume, do not use military jargon or unit nomenclature. If unsure about your future profession or any of this information, check out The Transitioning Military Series at Gr8Transitions4U.com.

Once you have a profile, you will want to gain an advantage by finding civilian connections. A great way to start finding civilian connections is to join and participate in LinkedIn groups within your professional interest areas. This will allow you to view and learn from articles, postings and conversations with established leaders in your field; while enabling you to make important connections with people who are in positions to assist with your professional growth.

Free Linked in Premium Subscription: www.socialimpact.linkedin.com/programs/veterans/premiumform

As you physically meet other professionals during your transition, you want to make sure that you get connected on LinkedIn with them. Study their profiles and continue to expand your virtual network by requesting introductions to their connections within your career field.

As a military member or transitioning service member, you are entitled to additional LinkedIn capabilities that will help you expand your virtual network quickly. LinkedIn's commitment to the US military and veterans is demonstrated through providing the "Job Seeker Career Premium Subscription" free of charge for one year. Consider writing a good personal letter to professionals you connect with online. You will not get a response from everyone, but you can make some strong virtual connections in this manner.

You will often find free online seminars for a myriad of topics on transition and professional development. Take advantage of these, which are often given for the cost of an email address – so that they can announce future events.

As a final note, communicate and build upon your virtual network and relationships. Do not be afraid to ask your connected professionals for career field advice or assistance. Generally, civilians are interested in helping military members make a smooth transition into the corporate world. Allow your connections to know your desires and concerns. Let them know how much you appreciate their input. This dialog will strengthen your virtual relationship with these professional connections over time.

So, have you started building your virtual network yet? Try some of the following links in this table.

Linkedin Professional Groups	
Construction Project Management	https://www.linkedin.com/groups/3776031/
PMI Project, Program, and Portfolio Management	https://www.linkedin.com/groups/2784738/
C, Linux and Networking	https://www.linkedin.com/groups/3067360/
PMI® Military Liaison	https://www.linkedin.com/groups/6798540/
US Military Veterans Network	https://www.linkedin.com/groups/50953/
Logistics Network	https://www.linkedin.com/groups/147489/
US Army Transitioning	https://www.linkedin.com/groups/4059941/
Woman Owned Small Business - WOSB	https://www.linkedin.com/groups/2489151/
Security Clearance Jobs - ClearanceJobs	https://www.linkedin.com/groups/78232/
Veterans Hired	https://www.linkedin.com/groups/3754418/
Veteran Job Opportunities	https://www.linkedin.com/groups/4130945/
Project Transition USA	https://www.linkedin.com/groups/4842096/
I want to be a PMP®	https://www.linkedin.com/groups/2356441/

- Do you have a professional Networking account?

- Have you created a professional profile with a picture?

- Have you researched the company and employees from the organizations you are/will be interviewing with?

- Have you looked on social media and your professional network for those employees and leaders? Do you know where they went to school? Did any of them serve in the military?

6.3 Cb - Branding

Building a brand is essential. In today's entrepreneurial environment, every individual is a brand. But what is a personal brand? Branding is the act of consciously and intentionally creating and influencing the perception of yourself by positioning within your desired or given field. This is done by elevating your personal credibility and differentiating yourself from the others along a path of career advancement, increasing influence and your personal impact.

You will want to try to make your "brand" widely recognized, providing a homogenous look and perception of yourself. The brand showcases your experience, expertise, competencies, and achievements within a community of interest or industry/marketplace. Your competitors understand branding, and they are consistently developing and refining their personal brand.

This starts by ensuring you have a uniform message to send to the community through all your professional marketing materials, such as resumes, online professional networking presence, and cover letters. Additionally, you want nothing to take away from your credibility, such as negative comments or postings on the internet or social media. All of this takes work.

Many military service members already have LinkedIn accounts. Unfortunately, many of these accounts just gather dust. When wanting to leverage and unleash the powerful capabilities of this platform for more dynamic personal branding, the question is often asked "What should I do next?"

So, let's talk about establishing your professional brand. Start with the headline and the summary, which provided tremendous personal brand visibility allowing you to be found and enhancing professional relationships. The headline is the sentence next to your name. This is the summary in a profile section where you can tell your professional story – where you have been, where you are, and where you would like to go in your career. Think of it as a 'snapshot' that tells your professional story. You need to assume the reader will never read another word about you and that this headline is all they will see…and you begin to get an idea of the weight of the headline and the importance of getting it right. This is your 15-second commercial, your billboard…if people yawn while reading it, go back to the drawing board.

The headline can contain up to 120 characters. Rather than simply typing in your rank, unit, and military position, you need to take time to translate these elements to a specific civilian job title that can be understood by the prospective employer. Use keywords to describe your professional strengths, as these are the words others type into LinkedIn when searching for someone with your skills and abilities.

Things to work on, remove all military jargon, acronyms, unit names, and phrases unfamiliar to the public to better communicate with non-military people who may be reading your profile and considering hiring you. No recruiter, hiring manager or potential connection wants to guess, or feel "stupid" for not knowing.

It is possible to land hoped-for positions through LinkedIn or other professional networks. Remember, LinkedIn is a giant search engine, like Google. People find you by typing in keywords related to the types of skills they are looking for. Your job in using LinkedIn to create greater professional visibility is to think about which words, terms and phrases a recruiter or any LinkedIn member might type in to find someone like you and use those keywords. The better you match with their expectations the more opportunities will come your way.

Make sure you display a great professional picture. You will want people to see you as a civilian. Choose a location (e.g. "Greater Baltimore area"). If you are currently stationed in a location where you do not plan to live post-military, state your desired or future location.

Within your brand, speak as yourself, not in 3rd person. If you want recruiters to contact you, say so. Clearly state your professional strengths and experiences. Line them up with core deliverables for the job you want. Do not use "Transitioning" or "Retired" in your headline, but you can use it in your summary. And finally, check your spelling.

Consistently and constantly work on your brand. Post interest information as it will help others and attract recruiters. Recruiters watch LinkedIn and other sites, so the more active you are the more your profile will be looked at. For additional reading on branding, check out Gary Vaynerchuk's *Crush It!*

- What is a personal brand? Do you have one? Does your resume reflect the brand?

- What are the steps you need to take to establish a brand within your sector?

- Does your online profile match your resume? Are your goals and objectives synchronized?

- Have you sanitized all of your documents of any military terms?

6.4 Cs - Shadow

When you transition from the military, keep your eyes and ears open for job shadowing opportunities. Experiencing a workplace first-hand enables you to learn much more about a career than performing an extensive internet research. It is an awesome experience for a transitioning service member; assuming you can find an opportunity. It is not easy, so let us take a look at few thoughts on how to land a shadowing opportunity.

The question is "Who am I going to shadow?" Ideally, you will want to find someone who is in the same type of job you think you would like to have or a position that you desire to obtain in the near future. Find a company, organization, or profession you think you would like to pursue. Again, this takes some personal reflection and study. Target places and organizations, you would like to be with.

Job shadowing is a tremendous opportunity for you to observe or "shadow" someone doing their job, in their workplace environment. A job shadow can be as simple as an hour-long visit with one person. Or, if you are fortunate, you may be able to land a week-long experience where you can interact with numerous staff members and observe a variety of activities. Perhaps you can see how different departments behave and interact with each other.

Ideally, the best time to shadow will be prior to your departure from the Service. However, you may not be able to find an opportunity until after you have departed. Further, you may find that you have already obtained a job after the military, but you are disenchanted. Regardless of timing, take the opportunity to shadow if it is afforded.

You learn so much about a company through experiencing them in the trenches. If you already know the career field you want to pursue, job-shadowing can reveal inside information about the company culture, atmosphere, and attire. Narrow your search to the department level by shadowing people or observing different departments of the same company to see various environments. Do not underestimate your ability to gain friends and professional connections.

Finding an opportunity can be tough. Before you try setting up a job-shadowing experience on your own, investigate resources in your area for this kind of activity. Check into local or state government agencies that offer such programs. Sometimes companies publicly announce job-shadowing programs. More often they are announced through special programs. Some military transition assistance programs help find shadowing opportunities. A few to consider are:

- **DoD Skillbridge:** If you are within 180 days of transition, look at DoD Skillbridge (**https://dodskillbridge.usalearning.gov/**) as they partner with private industries to help veterans find jobs, but also aid companies find the workforce that they need for their industries.

- **FourBlock:** FourBlock.org is great transition organization offering a series of great services through a comprehensive suite of in-person and online career readiness programming for veterans.

- **Hiring Our Heroes Fellowship:** This is an innovative 12-week program that provides **transitioning service members** with professional training and hands-on experience in the civilian workforce, and prepares candidates for a smooth transition into meaningful civilian careers. https://www.hiringourheroes.org/fellowships/

If you cannot locate an opportunity using these methods, find someone in "career development" in an organization or profession you think you would like to pursue. Ask for an informational interview, where you might come to an organization to learn more about the company and its processes. Request information on their referral process and if job shadowing opportunities exist. Explain why job shadowing interests you and request their procedures for entering such a program.

If you get to an informational interview and you hit it off with the interviewer, you might ask if you can come back to spend some more time with your interviewee in a job-shadowing situation.

If you get the opportunity to job shadow, ask questions, but don't bombard the professional with too many. Let them do the talking. Be open to meeting as many people as possible during the experience. Ask them if they know others in similar jobs that you might shadow. Many have veterans as co-workers that would be willing to assist.

Treated well, the professional you are shadowing may become a valuable member of your civilian network. Remember that they have made a significant investment by spending time with you, so stay in touch with them and make sure you send them a thank you note.

Very few get to experience a job shadowing opportunity. You can increase your chances through proactive networking for opportunities. The time spent shadowing is invaluable and well worth your investment.

- Is there a shadowing opportunity for you?

- Is this something you would enjoy?

- Can you shadow during your transition?

6.5 Ct - Temping

I have been asked, "Should transitioning service members take a temporary job?" The bottom line, it depends on your situation. Here are some thoughts.

It is often challenging to find a job straight out of the military. A friend of mine recently asked, "It seems unfair. How do I get the experience needed to apply for a job, when no one will hire me without experience?"

Everyone has their own set of employment challenges when they leave the Service. It has become increasingly difficult in recent years to make an easy transition, especially for younger service members.

Therefore, you may need to consider what many guardsmen and reservists have known for years! Between active-duty stints and going to school, many of these young warriors are resourcefully finding solutions to this challenge using a temporary agency. As you transition from the service, do not exclude the idea of finding a temporary position while looking for the right permanent job. Here are a few reasons you may want to visit a temporary agency during your military transition.

Good news. Temporary agencies are paid by filling positions. You will have someone assisting your post military job search, the moment you walk through the door. If you are willing to accept the job and the pay, you can go to work quickly. Keep in mind, if you are not satisfied you can find another temporary position and/or agency if needed.

A temporary job will get you out of the house and provide activity, both leading to a sense of hope during your transition. Most would agree that "A" job is better than "No" job as it improves the psyche and is far better than sitting at home trying to figure out how to make ends meet on a tight budget.

By temping, you gain exposure to job seekers, supervisors, and other employees. This will increase your personal network outside the military. Talk to these folks about their experiences. You may gain valuable information and contacts from the knowledge they provide. This knowledge may potentially enable you to set your sites on other positions inside and out of the organization. Remember, your military friends are great, but most will not have the contacts to help you find a commercial position.

You will learn new job skills, increase your personal capabilities, and enhance your resume. This is a great way to boost your knowledge, skills and attributes while gaining commercial job exposure if you are not quite sure where you want to work after your military experience.

As a transitioning service member, temping allows you to learn more about commercial companies and what you like and do not like in work environments. It gives you time to figure out your post military direction, enabling your next career move.

Temporary jobs often develop into permanent jobs. As a service member, you know how to get the job done and work hard when the situation dictates. Taking a temporary job may land you a permanent position with the company.

Getting to work quickly will enable you to size up the competition. You will meet folks that are struggling, employees that are doing well and others that are facing similar challenges to your own. Talk to everyone and learn what they have going on in their lives. This will increase your knowledge of the commercial market and how to survive your military transition.

On the downside, there are often minimal benefits with a temporary position. There is no commitment by the temp agency or hiring organization. The temp agency is concerned about follow on business with the hiring organization, while the hiring organization is using a "try before they buy" approach with their temporary employees. Due to these factors, temporary work is on the rise in the US; while temporary job duration is growing. As a transitioning service member with the right perspective and "can-do" attitude, both dynamics will work to your advantage.

Think positively. You are not alone. Most veterans experience challenges and employment problems during their transition from the military. Like the millions of veterans that have already walked this path, you will find the right job. But while you are looking, do not rule out temporary work. It could provide a path to a permanent and lucrative future position.

- Is there a stigma with temporary work? Have you considered temporary work as a stop gap?

- Might you be forced to take temporary work? Can you think of a reason to take temp work when not forced?

- Are you prepared to temp – if needed to get by?

Post-Transition Factors

Professial Development

You are now in the post transition phase. You have found a great job. Congratulations! Now is the time to grow into a great employee. Just like the military, you must continue to develop professionally.

As mentioned earlier, you will need to reinvent yourself every few years to remain viable. In this section we are going to talk about different pieces of the professional development pie. These elements should remain at the forefront as you progress and learn more about your day-to-day job. Remember, never be afraid to engage management about your personal professional development.

7.1 Dm - Finding a Mentor

Do you have a career mentor? We often speak of mentorship in the military. As you begin your military transition journey, having a mentor is a critical factor in finding a great job in your desired career field! You may have someone you think is a great mentor for your military transition, but how do you know if they will be able to provide transition assistance and guidance? Before you begin your search, take some time to think about what you are trying to acquire from a career mentor. A mentor is informal and long-term.

First, find someone that is honest and cares about YOU. This can be intimidating. Realize that this is going to be an intimate relationship, as the mentor needs to know YOUR strengths and weaknesses. They must be willing to point and give suggestions for personal improvement areas.

Second, your mentor should be someone that you can reach out to, who is willing to listen and advise when needed. Your career mentor should be aware of your interview activities and they should be a great sounding board when things do not go as well. Finally, your mentor should be able to help you create actionable objectives while assisting you in achieving your career goals and milestones.

If you are behind in some specific areas, you may need coaching, education or training. This should not be confused with mentoring. You may have to pay for coaching, which is more formal and structured.

Third, your mentor should know the career field that you are pursuing. They should be able to identify resources that might provide opportunities and skills for your professional training. As you get close to transition, the utility and availability of your uniformed mentors will diminish. They will be busy performing their military mission. Further, they may not have the knowledge required to provide essential transition and career field guidance for you. Therefore, you will want to find a civilian who is working in the career field that you desire to get into.

Fourth, if you do not know anybody that would be a qualified mentor, then you need to get busy and join a networking organization. These organizations have a tremendous number of great professionals, willing to get involved in your life. You will find these professionals in local organizations like Toastmasters, Rotary, Kiwanis Club, and the Optimists Club. Additionally, look for and join local career field specific groups of interest, such as the Project Management Institute (PMI), Microsoft Azure or Project Server User Group, a Scrum Alliance community group, or the American Academy of Medical Administrators (AAMA). If you are a military engineer, consider a local chapter of a state or national society for engineers.

Getting involved with these organizations not only enhances your knowledge and professional capabilities, it also increases your network. The biggest windfall of your network is interacting with seasoned professionals, many of whom are more than willing to mentor you during your current job hunt and provide guidance for your future career. Many of these professionals genuinely desire to help, as they are veterans or veteran friendly!

Finally, when entering a mentor relationship, take a long-term approach. Understand your mentor may provide invaluable guidance for years to come and perhaps become a lifelong friend. To find a great mentor will take work and effort on your part; however, the payoff is priceless.

- Do you have a mentor in the military? Is this concept foreign?

- Have you thought about what a mentor might assist you with?

- Do you know anyone in the career field you desire to work in? Have you approached them?

- What organizations could you join and meet professionals in the career you desire?

7.2 Dp - Path Analysis / Job Hopping

As you progress in your post-military career, carefully consider the pros and cons of job hunting. Recruiters and hiring managers understand corporate longevity is a rare commodity. However, unexplained job-hopping can be detrimental to employment. Do you have a career path? Have you done the diligence to determine the best road for your successful growth?

Many find waiting for the next performance review and hoping for a salary increase, an unsatisfactory method for professional growth. You may be tempted to leave your company and quickly move to more challenging positions with higher salaries. In the short term, you may gain thousands of dollars, but you may damage relationships or burn bridges along the way. The immediate gain may not outweigh the hazards or be the best path for your career. Job-hopping may seem a reasonable tactic for career growth but take time to understand the benefits and challenges.

First, job-hopping is not always frowned upon. The job-hopping pattern is more readily understood in younger, less experienced employees and professionals. Two to three years at one job is not uncommon for employees under the age of 35. Further, there are some occupations that job-hopping is both beneficial and completely understandable, such as traveling nurses or project managers. Additionally, job-hopping can be desirable in such career fields as IT. When an IT specialist changes companies or locations, they gain more knowledge about various environments, cultures and technologies. These professionals must stay current and they can do this through training and a variety of experiences.

Unfortunately, red flags occur when you are an experienced mid-level employee, with an appearance of moving every year or two. The challenges are simple to understand. Hiring managers are often concerned with a resume portraying multiple short-term stints. Discerning whether you were let go or whether you left willingly becomes difficult. You may be perceived as disloyal or being unstable. Employers may perceive you as a poor investment, as your organizational allegiance may be questioned, or they may believe you could move on at the first sign of trouble. If job-hopping is your method for promotion and salary increases, it is essential that you can describe why you continually change jobs in terms acceptable to the hiring organization.

So, how do you work the job search, if you already have a choppy resume? With some preparation and a good explanation, job-hopping can be portrayed during an interview as a favorable situation. You just need to be able to describe your career progression to the hiring manager, when the question is asked.

Start by painting your experiences in a positive light, in your resume, cover letter and interview. When the inevitable question comes up, elaborate the positive aspects. Discuss how your experiences provide a diverse background, giving you exposure to different businesses and a wide range of leaders and managers. Tell the employer your varietal positions have made you unique, increasing both your knowledge and network. Let them know, your experiences have provided access to more information resources and exposed you to numerous opportunities, different types of jobs, work, and environments.

There are many benefits and challenges associated with the job-hopping resume. Without doing the appropriate level of homework and having the right answers for the tough questions, you may find the appropriate answer to be challenging and the interview daunting. However, if you are prepared and you can talk about the issues associated with your job-hopping experience, you should be able to sail through your next interview.

- We move on every year or two in the military. Do you think you will get tired of the same civilian job in a year?
- Is Job Hopping something you would intend to do? Are you concerned about the negative implications?
- What are the deciding factors for you, when deciding to move on to another position or company?
- Have you analyzed your resume for pitfalls? Are you able to discuss your resume challenges with a prospective employer?

7.3 Dv - Volunteering

As you transition to your first commercial job, reflect on how volunteerism is prevalent in the military. Service members are asked to volunteer, and leaders often ask for volunteers. At first glance, some say "What's in it for me?" However, experts state that volunteering is valuable and is a great way to continue your personal development.

Embracing a new challenge is a tremendous professional development experience in a package. Inevitably, you will be gaining new skills. You do not have to accept every opportunity, as you can volunteer yourself to death. However, when you have a new challenge at work, you can often grow your personal skills and abilities. Work is much more than an exchange of your time for money. You personally receive value through developing your personal skills on the job.

People are fired every day. You cannot count on your job forever. Few get to stay with the same organization for a career. You have heard many times, "Everyone is replaceable." Therefore, do not disregard opportunities. By accepting new challenges, you become more valuable to your employer. More than job security, your volunteering and acceptance of new challenges make the organization more valuable. Improving yourself enlightens those around you enhances the organization. Everyone knows and loves a helpful employee that cares as much about others' success as their own. Celebrate other's success through collaboration and you will be helping to make the organization more successful.

Your military training taught you that the mission is about people. Through collaboration, co-workers provide great ideas. We know that people are the most important resource in any project. Binding collaboration effort and the people together is a relationship. Volunteering for a challenge will get you to work with other folks that you may not know very well or have never met. You may get to work with staff from other departments. You will gain appreciation and understanding for their work but also the organization at large.

Do not look at new challenges and volunteering with regards to time or number of tasks it will take, also look at the benefits of building new relationships. You never know, these relationships may be beneficial - not only for you during the effort, but perhaps in the future as well.

Finally, some employees go to work for a paycheck. Others are there because they love the work. If you feel like you are there marking time, take on a new challenge as soon as possible - for your own personal satisfaction with work. Nothing is worse than enduring - day in and day out the same old boring tasks. Volunteering for a new challenge at work will give you energy and perhaps enable others to grow as well. Nothing lasts forever, and roles and responsibilities change all the time. Therefore, you may be able to carve out new roles for yourself, especially if you liked the work you volunteered for.

You have a great idea for the organization? Make sure you volunteer to lead the effort. Perhaps there is a role for you to grow and learn new skills, make new relationships, and enhance your personal job satisfaction through volunteering. Remember, high performers and achievers willingly volunteer all the time.

- Do you typically volunteer? Do you see the benefits?
- Are there some new challenges that lay ahead in your organization?
- As a leader, are you willing to step out and volunteer to push a new effort?

7.4 De - Engage Management

In the military, we knew how to talk with seniors. We would often seek out guidance on challenging situations and look to them for mentorship in our careers. Nothing is different in the civilian world. If you can have a good relationship with your boss, you are fortunate indeed. You will be happier at work, and able to engage them when times are professionally or personally challenging.

But what if you are one of the unfortunate ones? What if you have an exceedingly difficult boss, which happens quite often to many? How do you survive in a tough work environment? Now that you are no longer wearing the uniform, you can no longer be "voluntold." But you do need to have a method for dealing with crummy bosses. Here are a few pointers for working in a challenging environment.

In a classic risk mitigation effort, you have four methods: Avoidance, Acceptance, Control or Transference. Understand them and employ the methods from the start and save yourself some pain.

Avoidance - If a risk has unwanted negative consequences, you try to completely avoid the outcome. If you determine your boss is or is going to be difficult or the environment is going to be undesirable prior to your acceptance of the job, then you may need to make the tough call and not accept the position. If you are unsure during the interview, make sure to ask questions, which is always better than saying you have no questions.

Acceptance – But what if you accept the position and life is not good? This is a slippery slope. If you accept the position, know that every boss has good and bad days. If you believe the total number of good and bad days is no better or worse than anywhere else, then you have basically accepted the job / situation and said you will do the best you can. You may have decided the job is so good that you are going to stick it out and tolerate your boss - because they are providing employment and a means to an end or goal. However, if you start to think otherwise, you need to use another risk management method to regulate the risk.

Control or reduction - If it is not possible to reduce the probability or the severity of having a difficult boss, then you want to employ some form of control to reduce the potential damage. In theory it is the bosses' job to manage you. However, to survive, get the raises and promotions you deserve, you must learn to control your boss. You will need to try figuring out what your boss wants from you, as an employee. You must provide the communication and feedback they desire.

Be reliable through reaching goals and completing tasks on time. You can try to derive your pleasure from making the boss happy! Figure out what your boss does well and learn how they do this. Some say they learn more from bad bosses than good bosses; perhaps on how not to manage.

Transference – What if you cannot take it anymore? Transference means to shift the burden of risk or consequence to another party or in this case, move on! Sounds easy, but it is challenging. People linger in bad situations too long, for unfounded concerns. Even the most successful people do not win every battle. We must recognize that moving on from an unwinnable situation, is not a failure. Understand, toxic managers and environments cause stress and negativity. A bad job situation is not a good use of your time, energy, and will contribute to the destruction of your health. In this day and age, you need not be a martyr.

Moving on can be a bit dicey. Burn no bridges. If you can, make sure you find a job before you depart. Tell no one of your job search until you accept a new position. You may find, just making the effort to look for a new position can be a tremendous stress reliever. Remember, moving on is indicative of professional maturity.

- Have you found yourself with a difficult boss in the military?

- You can move on in a civilian job, you just need a plan. Have you thought of all the challenges associated with leaving a company?

- What would put you over the edge and make you want to move on from your current position?

- Is loyalty more important to you than your personal happiness?

7.5 Ds - Secrets of Success

You are an entrepreneur. Regardless of who you work for, you must remain viable and prepared to change with the times. Entrepreneurs know this, or they go out of business. Do not be blinded by reaching a steady state at work. Your corporate loyalty may appear beneficial, but it may actually be hurting you personally and professionally.

Long-term employment disappeared many years ago. Medium-term employment is arguably on its way out. Organizational tenure is becoming shorter and shorter. To make matters more complex, the longer you stay at a job, the less marketable you may become. You may see difficult interview questions like, "What did your seventh year with company X teach you, that you failed to learn earlier?" This doesn't mean there aren't benefits to making your relationship with your employer last. But it does mean you should be aware of how changing attitudes toward employment and tenure affect the job market.

Fortunately, there are methods to stand out in your company and be valued by your leadership. Further, there is a very personal and professional silver lining for yourself with each approach.

Remain Viable

This adage is true for your current employment situation and your personal professional development. Peter Drucker, a renowned business author, discussed this issue in detail. He stated years ago that to remain viable you must reinvent yourself every 3 or 4 years. Today, reinvention may need to occur even more often. You remain viable by staying well informed, learning new skills, applying them and continuing to improve your resume. Most importantly, be prepared to move on when the timing is right.

Take Initiative

This is true for work and yourself. Don't wait. You have often heard that giving the extra 5% can make all the difference. Do it for yourself professionally and on the job site.

Network and Build Rapport

Find other people in the organization that are doing different types of work. You may find what they are doing interesting. You can help them, learn from them and grow your professional network at the same time.

Perform Business Development

Your company needs you to grow their business. This is true at all levels. If you find a way to increase corporate work share, save dollars through new business relationships or find a new line of work for your company, you are playing an instrumental financial role, while enhancing your organizational viability. If your company is not interested in your discoveries, you have learned during the process and may inadvertently find another great opportunity for yourself.

Be a Team Player

Be willing to help others whenever you can. This is good for yourself, the team, the company and your future. You may be learning new skills, or you may just be supporting others and their great ideas. Either way, there is significant personal growth and development opportunity for both yourself and the company. And you solidify new and existing relationships.

The value you bring to your employer is the basis of your employment. If you don't value your contribution, they may not either. Learn, grow, and remain engaged and you will be providing viability to the company. However, the largest dividend may very well be the enhancement of your personal growth and development. When the time to move on arrives, you will be confident and prepared!

- Do you understand your employer's expectations?

- Do you keep the knowledge to yourself or do you share it?

- Do you seek ways to improve the situation at work?

- Do you look for the win for everyone, when considering the way ahead?

- Are you Team Player? How willing are you to take on extra duties?

- Are you willing to make recommendations and lead the effort if desired?

A Final Note of Encouragement

I want to thank the thousands of transitioning military personnel that have purchased and used books from the Transitioning Military Series. It is my personal desire that each of you have highly satisfying and successful civilian career. After all, you deserve it. You have Served selflessly, worked tremendous hours, enjoyed and/or suffered numerous deployments and numerous difficult days. Most have done this willingly without reservation. Now it is your turn to advance to the next challenge – you post military career. I trust you will find the materials in *The Periodic Table of Military Transition* helpful and insightful.

Acknowledgments

I am extremely grateful for the opportunity to publish again on this very important subject. I have numerous thank for assistance with this book. First, I thank God for allowing me to complete this task. Covid, multiple moves, retiring for second time are just some of the personal challenges that I faced during the publication of this book. Second, my wife has been patient as I have continued to pursue this line of work. Being a veteran, Human Resource Specialist, and helping many Service members along the way, Kellie knows the importance of successful military transition.

I am thankful to Tamara Parsons of Kensington Type for her diligence and assistance in production of this book. Sandy Lawrence's solid incouragement and the numerous reviews by Dawnn McCullough, Cindy Gadis, Al Calvi, Cam Miles, Noel Fleming and Bill Baxter were instrumental to this publication. Thank you all!

Finaly, I am the very proud father of two veterans that have successfully made military transitions. Both of these men provided currency, kept me up-to-date through conversation and insight into the current military and transitional envorionment.

The Transitioning Military Series

The Transitioning Military Series helps service members evaluate and understand their potential to transform themselves into a marketable commodity within both public and private sectors. Each career-based book enables the translation of military experience to the commercial world. Read and use each of these books as a reference to guide during your transition.

A unique combination of features offered through this book series include:

- Career Mapping and Translation
- Transitional Preparedness
- Personal Strategic Roadmap
- Commercial Market Exploration
- Individual Assessments
- Transition Success Stories

Interested in another career field? Check out our other books on career field transition for the military from Gr8Transitions4U.

Project Manager

Logistician

IT Professional

Cybersecurity Professional

Combat Arms Professional

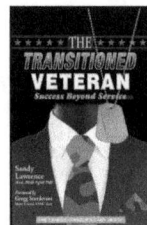

Transitioned Veteran

Jay Hicks is dedicated to providing insight and guidance for those looking to transition successfully from the Military with the least amount of stress. Jay speaks around the U.S. in support of transition as well as career field insight, and are available for conferences, podcasts, webinars, and training. For more information on upcoming events and new releases, visit: GR8Transitions4U.com.

www.ingramcontent.com/pod-product-compliance
Lightning Source LLC
Chambersburg PA
CBHW071100090426
42737CB00013B/2400